Sales Questions That Close Every Deal

Sales Questions That Close Every Deal

1,000 FIELD-TESTED QUESTIONS TO INCREASE YOUR PROFITS

Gerhard Gschwandtner

with Donald J. Moine, Ph.D.

McGRAW-HILL

*New York   Chicago   San Francisco   Lisbon   London   Madrid   Mexico City
Milan   New Delhi   San Juan   Seoul   Singapore   Sydney   Toronto*

The **McGraw·Hill** Companies

1 2 3 4 5 6 7 8 9 0   DOC/DOC   0 9 8 7 6

ISBN-13: P/N 978-0-07-147588-4 of set
               978-0-07-147864-9

ISBN-10: P/N 0-07-147588-5 of set
               0-07-147864-7

McGraw-Hill books are available at special quantity discounts to use as premiums and sales promotions, or for use in corporate training programs. For more information, please write to the Director of Special Sales, Professional Publishing, McGraw-Hill, Two Penn Plaza, New York, NY 10121-2298. Or contact your local bookstore.

DISCLAIMER OF LIABILITY

Selling Power, Association for Human Achievement, Dr. Donald Moine, and Gerhard Gschwandtner hereby state that the sales questions in this book are being presented for illustrative and training purposes only. No liability is assumed or taken for any use or misuse of these sales questions. Do not use any questions or statements contained in this book without prior approval of your management or legal department. Never say anything that is not true for your company or for your products or services.

TO YOUR SUCCESS!

Research shows that

- 80 percent of all salespeople do not prepare a list of carefully phrased questions in advance of a sales call.

- 90 percent of all questions asked by salespeople during the average call are *closed* questions.

- The top sales producers use their own personal sales questioning strategy based on open questioning techniques.

- The majority of lost sales opportunities happen because of the salesperson's failure to uncover the prospect's specific needs.

- Most sales training courses do not cover the subjects of questioning techniques and questioning strategies in their curriculum.

Contents

Acknowledgments   *xiii*

How to Get the Most Out of This Book   *xv*

How to Use This Book   *xvii*

How This Book Is Organized   *xix*

How to Ask Your Questions   *xxi*

CHAPTER 1: Opening Questions   1
            Opening with Benefits   2
            Stating Call Purpose   10
            Building Rapport   15
            Acquiring Cooperation from the Receptionist   21

CHAPTER 2: Qualifying the Prospect   25
            Identifing Reasons for Buying   26
            Determining Financial Ability to Buy   30
            Determining Customer's Authority to Buy   33
            Determining Timetable for Purchase   37
            Determining Competitive Situation   41

CHAPTER 3: Probing for Prospect's Needs   45
            Finding Your Prospect's Expectations   46
            Identifying Buying Motives   54
            Understanding Key Words   59

CHAPTER 4: Presentation Questions   63
            Feedback on Features and Benefits   64
            Trial Closes   72

CONTENTS

CHAPTER 5: **Handling Objections with Questions**   **81**
　　　　　　　Isolating the Objection   82
　　　　　　　Understanding Reasons Behind the Objection   86
　　　　　　　Answering Objections with Questions   90

CHAPTER 6: **Closing Questions**   **97**
　　　　　　　Alternative Closes   98
　　　　　　　Assumptive Closes   101
　　　　　　　Summary Closes   105
　　　　　　　Extra Incentive Closes   109
　　　　　　　Impending Event Closes   112
　　　　　　　Conditional Closes   115
　　　　　　　Direct Closes   120
　　　　　　　"Yes-Set" Closes   125

CHAPTER 7: **Upselling Questions**   **131**
　　　　　　　Upselling Questions   132

CHAPTER 8: **Referral Questions**   **143**
　　　　　　　Referral Questions   144

CHAPTER 9: **Follow-up Questions**   **151**
　　　　　　　Level of Satisfaction   152
　　　　　　　Product Performance   155
　　　　　　　Service/Maintenance   159

CHAPTER 10: **Tested Questioning Techniques**   **163**
　　　　　　　The Apology Question   164
　　　　　　　The Benefit Question   167
　　　　　　　The Checklist Question   170
　　　　　　　The Common Grounds Question   172
　　　　　　　The Comparison Question   175
　　　　　　　The Compliment Question   178
　　　　　　　The Conditional Question   180
　　　　　　　The Confidential Question   183

The Confirmation Question	186
The Definition Question	189
The Expectation Question	192
The Experience Question	194
The Explanation Question	197
The Fact-Finding Question	200
The Feeling Question	202
The Future Prediction Question	205
The "Good Reason" Question	208
The Hesitancy Question	211
The Humorous Question	214
The Imagination Question	217
The Importance Question	220
The "Just Suppose" Question	223
The Narrow-Down Question	226
The Opinion Question	229
The Optimistic Question	232
The Pessimistic Question	235
The Polite Question	238
The "Prime-the-Pump" Question	241
The Pro-and-Con Question	244
The Rephrasing Question	247
The Rhetorical Question	250
The Thought-Provoking Question	253

Acknowledgments

At this time, we would like to give credit where credit is due. This book is the result of eight years of research by *Selling Power* magazine and the sales psychologists at the Association for Human Achievement in Palos Verdes, California. However, this book could not have been written by any one person. We were able to assemble the book only with the assistance and expertise of the following sales teams we have had the privilege of consulting with and speaking to. We would like to thank the top salespeople working for the following companies for their help:

Adams-Cohen Brokerage
Anabolic laboratories
AnchorPad, Inc.
AT&T Communications
AT&T Information Systems
Baltimore Life Insurance
Blue Cross/Blue Shield
Castolin + Eutectic (Europe)
Control Data Corp.
Dave Del Dotto
   Productions

General Motors (GM)
Home Federal Bank
E.F. Hutton
IBM Australia
Isuzu Motors
Paine Webber
Scheduling Corp. of
   America
Shopsmith, Inc.
Toshiba Medical Systems
Valeron, Inc.

ACKNOWLEDGMENTS

Delphi Systems
Epson America, Inc.
First Federal Savings and Loan
  (Australia)

Veteran's Network
  of Homes
Zond, Inc.
Zurich Life Insurance

We would also like to thank Linda Seard and Laura B Gschwandtner for their invaluable editorial assistance.

How to Get the Most Out of This Book

We believe that you will derive many benefits from using *Sales Questions That Close Every Deal*. Studies, interviews, and advice from more than one hundred of the top sales forces in America and around the world, have determined the specific kinds of questions that highly successful salespeople ask that less successful salespeople don't ask, or ask much less frequently.

The power of questions has been known for several thousand years. The Bible states, "Ask and ye shall receive." All great communicators ask questions. Yet, until now, there has never been a book of the most powerful and effective sales questions.

We have found that the ability to ask appropriate, friendly, yet penetrating questions is usually acquired only after years of hard study and work. One of the benefits this unique book offers is that of *saving you time*. If you had a top sales pro accompanying you on every sales call, he or she would likely remind you to use questions such as the ones contained in this book. *Sales Questions That Close Every Deal* will help you to be your own sales coach.

How to Use This Book

Before any important sales call, review the appropriate sections of this book. Once you are acquainted with this book and its sections, a 10-minute review can prepare you for most sales calls. You will probably find it the most valuable 10 minutes you spend all day! One of our students told us recently, "It is better to spend 10 minutes working with this book than it is to spend an hour worrying about a blown sales call!"

If it is your first sales call on a particular prospect, review the beginning sections of the book on how to open with benefits; how to use questions to state the call's purpose; how to use questions to build rapport; and how to get more cooperation from the secretary or receptionist. If you have already called on this prospect two or three times, you will find the sections near the end on feedback of features and benefits, trial closes, isolating objections, finding the real reasons behind objections, and closing questions to be the most useful and powerful.

Using this book strategically will save you a great deal of time and energy. You will appear much more focused and professional. You will appear very friendly, and yet you will not have to waste much time in idle chatter. You will be using the proven questioning strategies of sales champions. In 10 minutes of preparation, you will find at least one dozen sales questions you can use. Your sales call will be well balanced and you will double your chances for success.

Without hours and hours of practice, it is impossible to remember all the questions you should ask in a professional sales call. *Please think of this book as an external human memory device.* You will find it especially useful when you are tired or at the end of a day. It will make selling much easier and more fun because it will take much of the work out of preparation. You can easily get to and find exactly the kinds of questions you need.

In addition, we've included a customizable CD-ROM with this book. Use the questions on this CD-ROM to create tailored questions specific to the products and services you sell and to address the concerns of the typical customer you serve.

Since this book will save you energy, you will be able to make more calls than other salespeople in your field. And, in any field of sales, it is usually true that the salespeople who make the most *high-quality* calls make the most sales! Shouldn't that be you?

How This Book Is Organized

To get the most out of any book, you have to know how it is organized, and how to find what you need. This book is organized according to the steps most sales professionals go through in a sales cycle.

You will find the book starts with questions on how to open the sales call and then proceeds with five sections of questions on how to qualify the prospect. Next, you will find three sections of powerful questions on how to probe for the prospect's *true* needs.

There are two sections on presentation questions, followed by three sections on handling objections with questions. Next, you will learn how top salespeople use questions to close the sale.

After you have closed the sale, you have a *perfect opportunity* to prospect for new clients. This is just the right time to ask for referrals; included for you here are the many ways of doing that.

You also will find follow-up questions. The easiest person to sell in the future is someone you have sold in the past. Our follow-up questions will show you how to get more business out of your existing customers! There is also a section of proven questioning strategies on selling your customers higher quality and higher priced products and services. This will definitely add to your sales success and to your income!

Finally, you will find *more than 30 sections of different types of questions* in "Tested Questioning Techniques." This last chapter is designed to be an encyclopedia of different types of questioning techniques. You will find forms of questions to use for every occasion that are invaluable and irreplaceable!

This book was not meant to be exhaustive or totally complete. During our research, we collected over 5,000 different powerful questions. In assembling this book, we had to leave some of them out. *However, we think you will find the questions here to be a very broad and useful cross-section of those that top salespeople rely on and need most often.*

REMEMBER: If you use the questions that sales champions use, you will acquire the power of top sales professionals!

A final word on how this book is organized: You will notice that at the end of every section, there are a number of blank lines. Rather than try to include 5,000 questions and have this book weigh as much as a small child, we have left room for you to add a few of your own favorites. Or, you can use the CD-ROM to customize your own ongoing list of winning sales questions.

This book can never be complete, but, as you add more power questions to it, it will become more and more perfect. If you hear a great new question, write it down! If you don't, you might forget it. As you add more questions to the appropriate sections of this book, as you get more involved with it, it will become part of you.

A tool is only effective if you use it. By writing in this book, you will mentally own it. Its contents will become part of your brain, part of your subconscious mind, and you will find yourself effortlessly coming up with brilliant questions where other salespeople would stumble!

How to Ask Your Questions

It is not enough, however, to know what questions to ask; sales-people must also know how to ask those questions. You can have the most powerful and focused questions in the world, but if you ask them in a mumbling voice they won't be effective. If you ask them like a drill sergeant, you won't get the response you want. If you ask them in a fearful way, you won't get the information you need. How, then, should, a sales professional ask questions to get the maximum benefit?

First of all: Be friendly. There is no need to be harsh or abrasive. You can't scare people into giving you information. If you want long-term cooperation and agreement, you must have a personal credo of being friendly and likable.

Next, concentrate on how you ask the question. Be self-confident. Don't be embarrassed or fearful. In some businesses, you have a perfect right to ask all the details of someone's net worth, their personal finances, income, etc. (in financial planning, for example). In some health care areas, you have a perfect right to ask about intimate details of how someone takes care of their body. In fact, if you don't ask the questions you need to ask, you aren't doing your job. If you don't ask these questions, you won't be able to help your prospect. So, don't be embarrassed. Be self-confident.

Talk the way your customer talks. Research shows that we trust people who talk like we do. We like people who are like us. We all think we are normal.

With fast talkers, speed up your voice just a little. They think it is natural and normal to talk quickly. If you speak slowly, they might suspect you are slow mentally. With slow talkers, slow your voice down when you ask questions. *Again, this will make them comfortable and they will think it is natural.* They won't know you are making any adjustment. All they will know is that they like you.

If your customer has a soft voice, do not raise your voice. Don't try to boom or project. A soft voice works best with a soft-spoken customer. Remember, we trust and like people like ourselves. Conversely, raise your voice slightly with a louder customer. Stronger people like other strong people. If you whisper, they might think you lack self-confidence.

A question is only as effective as the way it is presented. You can never miss by mirroring your customer's speaking patterns.

Finally, use your questions in a natural, normal way. Don't string together 20 or 30 questions in a row. The best sales calls are the ones that are conversational. Mix questions with small talk, with rapport building, with a little appropriate humor. Make your sales call a conversation between two friends. Take care of business, but be natural and never push the customer or make him or her feel uncomfortable.

If you master the contents of this book, if you learn what to say and then practice how to say it, we have no doubt this material will have a tremendous positive effect on your salesmanship and on your income. Remember, most salespeople don't prepare. It is no wonder that they do so poorly. The fact that you have already purchased this book puts you way out ahead of your competition. By using this book well, you will put yourself even further ahead. You will find yourself selling more and more with less effort and more fun.

CHAPTER
1

Opening
Questions

*Open questions open doors to new wealth you never
thought existed.*

- Opening with Benefits
- Stating Call Purpose
- Building Rapport
- Acquiring Cooperation from the Receptionist

Opening with Benefits

1. How would you like to *save $250 each month* in maintenance costs?

2. Would you like to know about a computer system that enables you to do professional quality typesetting and publishing for less than 10 percent of what outside services charge?

3. May I tell you about a machine that will be the envy of all your competitors?

4. Would you be interested in a way in which you could *increase your productivity by 23 percent*? Is that something we could discuss for about seven minutes?

5. Would you be interested in learning about a special sale we are offering next month to just a few of our customers?

6. You are always looking for ways to save time and money. That's the reason I brought a short video presentation that can illustrate the benefits of this new product in less time than I possibly could. Can you spare eight minutes now?

7. *People in your position are always looking for new ideas, especially ideas that can save money.* May I show you how our group health care plan can slash your health insurance costs by over 20 percent a year?

8. Would you like to learn about a nonsurgical procedure that can help your patients look *10 years younger*?

9. If there was a way of *paying for your child's college education for an investment of less than $25 a month*, would you be interested?

10. Would you be interested in a travel club that could save you up to 70 percent of all your airline tickets and 50 percent of your hotel bills?

11. May I show you a way of slashing your advertising budget by over 35 percent while at the same time increasing sales by 5 percent?

12. Would you like to know about a breakthrough in psychological testing that enables you to identify and select salespeople who could increase your company's performance?

13. If I could show you a product that has been rated outstanding by (industry publication), would you be willing to give it 10 minutes of your attention?

14. If I could show you a machine that could save your production department 20 percent in milling and grinding, would you be able to arrange for a demonstration with your president?

15. *If I could show you a way of making an extra $1,000 by Friday*, guaranteed, would you give me 10 minutes of your time today?

16. Would you feel more comfortable about investing the 15 minutes to discuss this opportunity if I promised to write a check for $100 in the name of your favorite charity if you decide you haven't benefited from our meeting?

17. Are you interested in owning the most beautiful car in the neighborhood?

18. Is a vacation for two on the most beautiful spot in Tahiti of interest to you?

19. Is being able to save over $10,000 during the next fiscal year of interest to you?

20. I see you are a professional. Would you like to own the most accurate and realistic audio system in the world today?

21. I assume you wouldn't mind finding a new way to save money, would you?

22. *If I could show you a way of saving over $7,000 in your manufacturing department, would you be willing to invest seven minutes to check out the facts?*

23. If I could show you a way of really impressing your boss, would you agree to a brief demonstration of this product?

24. I am sure you will be pleased to know that *we guarantee 99 percent uptime* of our system. Isn't that exciting news?

25. Have you heard about our *zero defects program*? It is the talk of the industry! Would you like to know how we do it?

26. Have you seen our brochure on the trade-in plan? Would you like to see how much money you could save?

27. What would be more interesting to you: *to save a small fortune in operating costs or have 99 percent availability*? [Wait for answer.] Well, I have good news for you.

Our new program offers you both. [Pause] Would you like to know how we do it?

28. Wouldn't it be great to have a machine shop that is the envy of all your competitors?

29. Have you ever seen a product in this field that just totally blew you away? Well, get ready! Take a look at our new...

30. Would you like to see something that is so exciting it will keep you up at night?

31. *What would it take to really amaze you?* [Pause] Well, get ready! Our new product was the hottest item at the industry trade show last week. Would you like to see it?

32. Are you sitting down? Well, get ready for some very exciting news! Are you ready?

33. Imagine your dream product. [Pause] Now imagine it is available at a price you can easily afford. Would you like me to tell you how we can make it available to you?

34. Let me ask you a question. Do you have a lot of willpower? [Wait for reply.] Well, you'd better have! When you see this new product, you will get the irresistible urge to put one on everyone's desk in your office.

35. _____
_____
_____

36. _____
_____
_____

Stating Call Purpose

1. The reason for my call is to help you with your _____ needs. Am I right in assuming that this is an area with potential for improvement?

2. My purpose at this time is to achieve a better understanding of your specific needs. Would you be kind enough to describe *the specifics* of your new plan, so I can develop a detailed proposal?

3. *My purpose at this time is to ask you a few questions that can help me understand your needs.* Would you mind if I asked them now?

4. Would you mind if I got your answers to a few questions, so that I don't make the wrong assumptions about your needs?

5. In the interest of saving you time with my presentation, could I get your feedback to a few questions?

6. To customize my proposal to your specific needs, may I clear up a few points with you?

7. To find out how I can be of best use to you and help you with your problem, may I ask you a few questions?

8. *I know that you are an expert in this field.* Do you mind if I ask you a few questions about _____?

9. *To make the best use of your time today* I'd like to ask you a few questions. Would you mind?

10. *To make sure I cover all the points that are of interest to you,* would it be okay if we reviewed a few questions now?

11. Before I begin my presentation would you please tell me the main points you are interested in?

12. Can we quickly review the purpose of our meeting today?

13. I want to assure you that all information I collect today will be kept strictly confidential. May I ask you a few basic questions about your needs?

14. My purpose for visiting with you today is to propose a new way to improve the productivity of your computer operation. *Is there anyone besides yourself who would be interested in learning about this innovation?*

15. I appreciate you taking the time out of your busy schedule to discuss your needs for improved service. *Could you tell me if there have been any changes since we talked last?*

16. Before we begin, could you tell me how your situation has changed since our last meeting?

17. It is always a pleasure to visit with you. *Can we start out by reviewing what we need to get accomplished? I have taken the liberty of drafting a brief agenda.* May I show it to you?

18. I know that you are pressed for time today. Could you tell me the three top features that you would want to get details on?

19. Could we quickly review what subjects you would like to cover today?

20. Obviously you have a busy schedule today. What would you like to get out of this meeting?

21. My purpose of this visit is to find a way to get you back as a satisfied customer. Is that a fair enough goal?

22. _____

_____

_____

23. _____

_____

_____

Building Rapport

1. Let me begin by saying that I really appreciate your interest in what we have to offer. What made you decide to give us an opportunity to serve your needs?

2. Are those your children in that picture? They are great-looking kids! What are their ages?

3. Is that your wife in the picture? What a beautiful lady. How long have you been married?

4. These are beautiful plants here in your office. How do you keep them in such great shape?

5. I see from the diploma on the wall that you went to _____. I really admire people with the diligence to complete advanced degrees. What did you major in?

6. These are beautiful offices. Did you select the furnishings?

7. *You look a lot younger than I thought you'd be.* If you don't mind my asking, how do you stay so young?

8. *I'm really impressed by your company.* You must have a lot of organizational ability.

9. Where did you get that impressive-looking sailfish?

10. *Everyone around here seems so happy.* What's your secret of keeping them motivated?

11. Every time I look at the paper, I read something great about your company. How do you keep growing at such an astonishing rate?

12. *I see that your company just won an industry award.* Congratulations. How did you manage to get it?

13. Are you still on the community hospital board? *I really admire people who put something back into the community.* How do you keep up with all these responsibilities?

14. *It amazes me how you manage to keep your desk so clean!* What's your secret?

15. People say that you are the most respected manager in the company. How do you do it?

16. I read the article about you in the trade newspaper. Congratulations! How do you get such great publicity?

17. Could you tell me how you manage to keep your calm under these trying conditions?

18. *Is that your golfing trophy?* What did you shoot to win it?

19. I have been looking forward to meeting you. I have heard that you are a real expert in antique cars. When did you start this hobby?

20. What is it that you like most about your job?

21. I bet that you have been traveling quite a bit. How many countries have you visited?

22. That's an interesting job title. Am I correct to assume that this is a new promotion for you?

23. That's an interesting name. Where does it come from?

24. Your company has an interesting name. Can you tell me the history of that name?

25. I always wanted to learn more about the beginnings of your company. Who was the founder?

26. Did you see the game last night? What did you think of _____?

27. It is a terrific day today. What kind of a rating would you give it on a scale of 1 to 10?

28. It's a beautiful day, isn't it?

29. Isn't it good to have rain for a change? We need the liquid sunshine, don't we?

30. I really like your reception area. It's so cheerful compared to the last place I visited. Did you know they had a sign saying: "We shoot every third rep; the second one just left?" [Say with a smile.]

31. While I was waiting for you, I learned something interesting from a magazine in your reception area. Do you know the meaning of the word "procrastinator"? Someone who can't take "now" for an answer. [Say with a smile].

32. As I was driving up to your office I was just wondering about how strange words are. Why is it that we drive on a "parkway" and park in a "driveway"?

33. _____

_____

_____

34. _____

_____

_____

Acquiring Cooperation from the Receptionist

1. Good morning. You may be able to help me. Could you possibly tell me *who* in your company makes the decision to purchase _____?

2. I hope I am not imposing on you, but could you answer a few questions to help me prepare for my meeting with your boss?

3. Just between you and me, is there any way I could get a two-minute interview with the president?

4. *You really know how to make someone feel welcome in your offices.* Would you be able to tell me who I should see about your company's printing needs?

5. I am positive that you won't mind helping me with finding the right person to talk to about purchasing safety equipment for your plant. Who would that be?

6. Excuse me. I am sorry to bother you, but I wonder if you could possibly do me a small favor?

7. I am sorry, I know how busy you are; however, I need to talk to your boss about an urgent matter. Could you call your boss right now?

8. Pardon me, you might be able to help me with this. Would you be able to find out when your sales manager will be back in the office?

9. Would you be gracious enough to tell your boss that I am calling to help with your computer needs?

10. Would it be possible for you to let your vice president know that I will wait in the hall until he or she is ready to see me?

11. I don't know if you realize how much is at stake for your company, but I really need to see your boss this morning. *When can you give me an appointment?*

12. I really appreciate your diligence. I wish my secretary was as diligent as you are. However, you don't need to worry. *Your boss will thank you for arranging this meeting.* This is an important business call. I hope you won't mind if I keep the details confidential, will you?

13. _____

_____

_____

14. _____

_____

_____

CHAPTER 2

Qualifying the Prospect

Not qualifying your prospects may not qualify you to close.

- Identifying Reasons for Buying
- Determining Financial Ability to Buy
- Determining Customer's Authority to Buy
- Determining Timetable for Purchase
- Determining Competitive Situation

Identifying Reasons for Buying

1. What purpose would this new product (service) have in your business?

2. What benefits do you expect as a result of making this purchase?

3. Congratulations for asking us to help you. For what special occasion are you making this important purchase?

4. I appreciate your interest in our _____. May I ask you what kind of use you had in mind?

5. Would you use this computer in *your home* or in *your business*?

6. May I ask you how this purchase fits into the *overall acquisition plan*?

7. Are you interested in *industrial grade* or *consumer quality*?

8. You know that we have a large selection. What kind of applications did you have in mind?

9. Are you considering Cadillac quality, or are you looking for Chevrolet standards?

10. Would you be interested in having this machine in your mining operation or would it be used as a backup for your quarry?

11. I assume you don't buy a _____ every day. May I ask what plans you have for using this _____?

12. I am pleased to hear of your interest in
_____. *What made you decide to get one?*

13. Ideally, what would you like to accomplish
with this purchase?

14. How did you hear about our company?

15. What interested you in our product line?

16. I appreciate your interest. What made you
decide to contact our company?

17. Of all the companies in this industry, what
made you pick ours?

18. Have you been looking for some time?
Why has it taken you this amount of time to
buy one of these?

19. _____

_____

_____

20. _____

_____

_____

Determining Financial Ability to Buy

1. I am sure that this is an important investment for you. Have you talked to your banker about financing?

2. Let's assume that you like what you see when I come to demonstrate our product. Would you be using your own funds for this purchase or would you be interested in hearing about our internal financing?

3. Have you thought about financing?

4. How do you plan on financing this purchase?

5. I am sure that you have thought about the financial aspects of this important purchase. *What are your expectations in this area?*

6. How is your *budget situation* at this time?

7. Are you comfortable talking about financing at this time, or do you feel that this is premature?

8. How have you historically handled the financing part of such a purchase?

9. What kind of budget have you set aside for this kind of purchase?

10. *Would you be needing help* with financing this purchase?

11. What type of *payment plan* would you be looking for?

12. Did you know that we offer a low-interest purchase plan? Would this appeal interest to you, or is this the kind of product you could buy with pocket change?

13. If you should decide to buy from us, what kind of financial assistance would you be looking for?

14. What kind of budget plans have you made for this investment?

15. _____

_____

_____

16. _____

_____

_____

Determining Customer's Authority to Buy

1.   Would you be able to tell me who in your company will be responsible for *signing the purchase order?*

2.   Who, other than yourself, is *involved in making the decision to buy* this product?

3.   I was wondering, is this type of investment decision made by a group of people in your company, or do you have the sole responsibility for approving this important purchase?

4.   What role will your immediate superior have in this purchase?

CHAPTER 2

5. Are you the only one with budget authority, or are there other individuals or groups involved in making this decision?

6. Is there anyone else, besides yourself, who will have a say in buying this product?

7. I realize that this is a big purchase. Would you mind telling me who will be the one *who has the final authority* to write the check for this purchase?

8. Normally this kind of purchase affects the entire family. If you don't mind my asking, how many people will be involved in the decision-making process?

9. Who else will be interested in reviewing a copy of our proposal?

10. Are you the one who is ultimately responsible for completing this transaction?

11. What role will your purchasing office assume in this acquisition?

12. Perhaps you could help me. What are the steps of your purchasing process, and how many people will be involved in making the decision?

13. I assume that this type of purchase is within your budget authority. Or am I making the wrong assumption?

14. Who else, besides yourself, has the authority to approve a purchase for this amount?

15. _____

_____

_____

16. _____

_____

_____

Determining Timetable for Purchase

1. When would you be needing this product in your facility?

2. When would you want to begin enjoying the benefits of this unique product?

3. Would this be for an immediate need, or are you planning this for later in the year?

4. When do you think you might be in the market for such a product?

5. How much in a hurry are you?

6. Will you be needing immediate delivery?

7. What kind of shipping dates did you have in mind?

8. Could you tell me approximately when you will be needing this product?

9. *Could you look at a calendar?* Would you be able to tell me your best estimate of when you will be needing this?

10. I was wondering about your timetable. *What are the steps you normally go through with this type of purchase?*

11. How fast do you need this?

12. What is the absolute latest delivery date you are looking for?

13. What kind of schedule would we have to meet to satisfy your needs?

14. By when would you want to have it?

15. Is early delivery important to you, or can you wait a few weeks?

16. Ideally, when would you like to have this machine ready for use in your operation?

17. What are your expectations in terms of time?

18. You sound like you are in a rush for this product. When would you have to have the first shipment?

19. Did you know that if you ordered today, we could get you the sale price and that we could arrange delivery for any time you wanted within the next four weeks?

20. _____

_____

_____

21. _____

_____

_____

Determining Competitive Situation

1. What other types of products have you considered that might satisfy your needs?

2. What other companies have you considered?

3. Just between you and me, *what other brands are you looking at?*

4. Do we have *any competition* at this time? Who?

5. Have you been looking at some of the other products on the market?

6. I was wondering, what other products have you already looked at?

7. You know better than I that there are many sources of supply. How many different suppliers are you willing to talk to?

8. How many companies are involved in this bid?

9. How many different suppliers have you asked *to submit a proposal*?

10. Are we the first company you have talked to? Who else is on the agenda?

11. You probably have talked with one or two competitors. That's to be expected. *What kind of impression did you get of their operations?*

12. I know that in this category we have no competition. Would you agree with this statement?

13. What other types of solutions have you considered that might solve your problem?

14. May I ask how many other companies we are competing with?

15. Who is our competition in this?

16. How many bids will you solicit?

17. What other companies are you considering that might possibly be able to satisfy your needs?

18. What other models have you looked at?

19. _____

_____

_____

20. _____

_____

_____

CHAPTER 2

CHAPTER 3

Probing for Prospect's Needs

In the same way that a doctor asks diagnostic questions to identify the real causes behind a patient's symptoms, the professional salesperson asks probing questions to identify the real needs behind the customer's wants.

- Finding Your Prospect's Expectations
- Identifying Buying Motives
- Understanding Key Words

Finding Your Prospect's Expectations

1. If there were an ideal solution to this problem, what would it be?

2. If I had a magic wand and I could give you the ideal product, what would it be like?

3. *What criteria have you set for evaluating* this type of product (service)?

4. What kind of service and support would you like to see to take care of your needs for the next five years?

5. *What do you expect us to do* to solve your problem in a way that will completely satisfy you?

6. What do we have to do to make you completely happy?

7. What type of features do you expect from a product like this?

8. Could you tell me the three top features you would like to see in this product?

9. What are the major benefits you are looking for?

10. I am sure you have given this purchase a lot of thought. What items have you put on your "wish list"?

11. Would you be able to tell me exactly what specific criteria you are looking for?

12. *Could you describe* the type of features you had in mind?

13. What are the most essential points we need to consider?

14. If you could get the machine of your dreams, what would it be like?

15. *If price were no object,* what would be the ideal solution to this problem?

16. What would your ideal computer *be able to do?*

17. Can you tell me all the features that you are *not* interested in having?

18. When you and your management team talked about that investment, what were the criteria that they felt were absolutely essential?

19. Is there anything at all we left off your list of features that you *need* to have?

20. Which price range best fits your budget?

21. What are your requirements in terms of financing?

22. Would you expect this to last a little longer than the one you purchased previously?

23. Ideally, what do you expect in terms of service?

24. What do we need to do to make you a *customer for life*?

25. What kind of price were you expecting to pay?

CHAPTER 3

26. What price range did you have in mind?

27. What sort of financing deal were you expecting?

28. What kinds of tax benefits are you most interested in?

29. Are you expecting us to arrange for shipping?

30. How much horsepower do you need?

31. Do you need extensive training, or just a brief orientation after delivery?

32. Were you planning to pay for this purchase all up-front, or were you planning to finance this purchase?

33. Do you expect to make a decision soon?

34. *For how many years* do you expect to use this product?

35. Are you planning to make this decision sometime this week?

36. *You know your operation better than me.* Would you share with me what your requirements are?

37. *How can we help you to avoid such a problem in the future?* What do you expect from us to solve your operator-training problems?

38. You are the expert in the company. *Based on all of your years of work with this company, what would you say you need to get the job done?*

CHAPTER 3

39. You know your company's financial position better than anyone. What would you say the budget is for an expenditure like this?

40. You are a known authority in this area. If you could get the perfect product, what would it look like? What would it be able to do without breaking your budget?

41. You know your company's policies better than anyone. How do they look at foreign manufactured goods? Do they expect this _____ to be 100 percent American made?

42. I trust and value your opinion. *What is the one thing, the one problem, we should avoid at all costs?*

43. Since we talked last, *what has changed in your expectations?*

44. _____

_____

_____

45. _____

_____

_____

Identifying Buying Motives

1. How much is this problem costing you now?

2. What would be the *consequences of not making this investment*?

3. What would happen to your productivity if you didn't buy this machine?

4. How important is it to you to *solve this problem quickly*?

5. How much longer can you put this off?

6. Is it important to you to get an *advantage over the competition*?

7. How important is it to you to own the very finest product available?

8. How important is it to you to get the most respected and most experienced company to support you?

9. You mentioned that quality is very important to you. I was wondering, why did you put "quality" on top of your list?

10. What is the most important reason that speaks in favor of buying this product?

11. Which *one of these three features* is the most important one to you?

12. What is it that you like about this product?

13. Without regard to price, *which model do you think is the best*? Why?

14. You mentioned that performance is important to you. What made you say that?

15. What would happen to you if you didn't make this investment?

16. Could you tell me how your operation will change as a result of having this product?

17. What is it that you like most about this type of machine? Why?

18. How important is it to you to have higher speed?

19. You mentioned that there were several requirements. *Which one is the most important to you?* Which one would you rank in second place?

20. When you look at maintenance costs and ease of operation, which of these would be more important to you?

21. Obviously price and quality are important. *Is there anything else that outweighs these two?*

22. Could you tell me your top two choices from this catalog? Why did you choose these?

23. I'd like to get your objective opinion on this. *What would you consider the strongest points of this product?* Why?

24. *It sounds like you are leaning* toward the larger model because the extra safety features are important to you. Am I reading you correctly?

25. _____

_____

_____

CHAPTER 3

26. _____

_____

_____

Understanding Key Words

1.   You mentioned that you are interested in "higher quality." What exactly do you mean by that?

2.   You told me earlier that you are looking for a "longer-lasting" product. How long would it have to last?

3.   You expressed an interest in "value." What kind of value are you looking for?

4.   You feel that a "stronger guarantee" is very important to you. What would you consider the essentials of a strong guarantee?

5.   You just used the term "reliability." Can you tell me exactly what "reliability" means to you?

6. Could you give me an example of what you mean by "more productive"?

7. What did you have in mind when you mentioned "easy access"?

8. You mentioned you had a need for a "better product." *Better in what way?*

9. I was wondering, *how do you measure "productivity"?*

10. How soon is "soon" to you?

11. How quick is "quick" to you? *How many days is that?*

12. What exactly do you mean by "lower interest"?

13. How long would you like this "extended payment term" to be?

14. When you say you want a "powerful" engine for this unit, how much horsepower do you need?

15. You say that your system should be "easy to expand." What do you mean by that?

16. You told me that you want a boat that is "easily transportable." How do you define that?

17. You mentioned that you would want to have a second unit "sometime in the future." How many years are we talking about?

18. You said that you wanted a "simple" product. How simple would it have to be?

19. You said that you would be willing to pay "a little extra" for the design. How much extra?

20. I remember your talking about your budget being "limited." What exactly do you mean by that? How much would you be able to invest?

21. You said that you would be interested "in larger storage capacity." How much square footage would you require to meet your needs?

22. _____
_____
_____

23. _____
_____
_____

CHAPTER
4

Presentation
Questions

When prospects are in the dark, orders will be light.
A feedback question after each feature presented will
increase your chances of closing the sale.

- Feedback on Features and Benefits
- Trial Closes

Feedback on Features and Benefits

1. How do you feel this machine will help you with your need for increased productivity?

2. Now that I have shown you this added feature, *can you see yourself using it?*

3. How would this feature be of use to you in your operation?

4. I'd like to get your *objective opinion* on this particular improvement. What do you think of it?

5. What specifically do you like about this new model?

6. When you looked at the specification sheet, *what items did you notice first?*

7. Would you mind telling me how you really feel about this feature?

8. *I sense that you are pleased with this feature.* How do you think you will be able to benefit from it?

9. Are you as excited about these new kitchen plans as I am? Isn't it great to have the convenience of fully automatic appliances?

10. I can't quite read you on that one. How does it appeal to you?

11. I am puzzled about that look. Are you seeing something that isn't quite up to your standards? Are you saying that you would rather have the deluxe model?

12. You seem happy about this latest improvement in our product line. Am I reading you correctly?

13. Would you mind sharing your honest feelings with me on this new product?

14. I sense that you are unsure about this. Why is that?

15. Are you comfortable with not having the top-of-the-line model?

16. Would you be able to tell me *what benefits you think this extra feature will bring you* in your particular situation?

17. Do you see any advantage in having faster turnaround?

18. Does it appeal to you to have *the most advanced engineering* available?

19. Is it important to you to have this extra guarantee? Why?

20. Have you thought about the status and the prestige you will enjoy from getting the very best? How do you feel about that?

21. How important is it to you to have the best warranty protection?

22. Now that we have seen how this works, could you tell me the three top features that would help you the most?

23. If I gave you the names of three major clients who are using this equipment right now, would you call them to find out how happy they are with it?

24. Just between you and me, how do you think your boss will react to having a model with these advanced features?

25. Would you mind telling me if there is *anything that needs to be added*? Is there any feature you need in addition to what we have planned for?

26. What do you think your president will say when he sees how much this product will boost your productivity?

27. How do you relate to having the very best?

28. What will your wife say about having the convenience of cruise control?

29. Am I correct in assuming that *this is what you had in mind*?

30. Does this feature meet your expectations?

31. How much money do you think this feature will save you in your operations?

32. Isn't this unique feature worth approximately a million dollars to your business in terms of increased productivity?

33. Don't you think that this feature alone could pay for the entire product?

34. Is it important to you to save money on maintenance? Can I show you how we do that?

35. How important is it to you to have easily accessible controls and higher comfort for the operator?

36. When you consider this feature, what does it make you think of?

37. Can't you see the savings that this feature will bring you? How much do you think you will be able to save compared to what you are paying right now?

38. I told you that this is a very special product. What do you think?

39. I have been doing most of the talking, and I appreciate your giving me your undivided attention. *May I ask you "at this point" for your objective opinion on this system?*

40. You have been very patient with me and I appreciate that. Now that we have seen the complete demonstration I'd like you to share something with me: *How many possible* *uses of our product can you think of in your operation?*

41. _____

_____

_____

42. _____

_____

_____

Trial Closes

1. In your experience, have you ever dealt with a supplier who would give you better backup than we are offering?

2. I am sure that you have had a lot of experience with budget negotiations. How would you go about getting this approved?

3. You seem to like this product. *I already see you using it* in your new facilities. Don't you?

4. How many of these do you think you will need in one year?

5. Let's assume that we could find a way of financing this purchase that does not create negative cash flow. Would you be interested?

6. Isn't that one more reason to *get the type of product you always wanted to own*?

7. Is there any reason why you shouldn't get the extra comfort and security?

8. Would you like it in blue?

9. The only question you need to ask yourself is: How many extra sales do I need to justify this investment?

10. The only questions you need to ask yourself are: Do I want to increase the productivity of my business? and, Can I afford the low monthly payments?

11. The only question you need to ask yourself is: Can I afford to wait and risk being overtaken by my competitors?

12. The only question you need to ask yourself is: Do I deserve the very best?

13. The only question you need to ask yourself is: Is this extra performance a good enough reason to justify this purchase?

14. I don't know how you feel about this, but aren't you getting tired of paying the repair bills for this old machine?

15. Suppose there was a system that would perform just as well as the one you saw demonstrated—but would cost 15 percent less. Would you be interested in having it installed?

16. If you had to choose between the one with chrome trim and the one without, which one would you pick?

17. Of the four samples I showed you, *which one is your favorite*?

18. Could you tell me your top three choices from this catalog?

19. It seems that you prefer the standard version. *Would you like me to find out if we have it in stock?*

20. It sounds like you are leaning towards the larger model. *Do you want me to find out the delivery schedule on this one?*

21. Let's assume for a moment that your partner will be as convinced of the benefits of this new model as you are. Would you then approve this investment?

22. Can you imagine for a second that there could be a way to enjoy having this product without a strain on your budget?

23. *If we can prove that this process works in your operation, do you think we will get the business?*

24. Suppose we could get the low-interest financing, would you order this month?

25. You seem pleased with the features of this computer. *Can you imagine using it?* Can you see how your productivity will go up?

26. You seem very enthusiastic about the performance data. *How can we transplant some of this enthusiasm to your boss* so we can get you one of these by next week?

27. You have been generous with your positive comments about the money-making other potential of this installation. *When would you like to begin enjoying these profits?*

28. You seem to be comfortable with this product. Do you feel as comfortable with the financing package?

29. You seem to be comfortable with the features. Do you feel as comfortable with the delivery date?

30. You seem to be pleased with what the product can do. Do you feel as pleased with your ability to meet the small payments?

31. You seem to be happy with having the latest model. Do you feel as happy with the protection provided in the service contract?

32. It sounds like you and I are in agreement with this: It is indeed superior to the other products you have looked at. *Am I reading you correctly?*

33. It sounds like we have covered all the bases. Let me ask you a question: What do we need to do to get your business?

34. It appears that you like this one. Would you like to talk to a few owners before you make this investment?

35. I like working with you on this project. What are the chances that your company will choose us as a supplier?

36. I like helping you with this plan, and I promise to continue to do so long after the project is completed. Let me ask you a question: On a scale of 1 to 10, how do you rank our chances for getting this contract?

37. Strictly off the record, is there any budget in your department we could draw on to cover the extra expenses so that you can get this training before the end of the year?

38. Just between you and me, is there any reason you would not get this improved model?

39. Isn't the extra power a good enough reason to install this one?

40. Isn't the advanced design a good enough reason to turn your competitors green with envy?

41. _____

_____

_____

42. _____

_____

_____

CHAPTER 5

Handling Objections with Questions

Every customer objection is a question in disguise. The only way to uncover the real question is to ask one.

- Isolating the Objection
- Understanding Reasons Behind the Objection
- Answering Objections with Questions

Isolating the Objection

1. *Is that the only reason* holding you back from owning this product?

2. Other than that, *is there any other reason* you can think of that would speak against this purchase?

3. Suppose that speed were not a problem. Would there be any other reason against installing this model?

4. Suppose we could solve the financing problem to your satisfaction. Would you go ahead with this purchase?

5. *Suppose we could find a satisfactory solution to this important concern of yours.* Would you give the go-ahead to this project?

6. *Just suppose we could solve the operating problem.* Would there be any reason against buying this machine?

7. Just suppose we could find a way to improve the quality. Would you ask us to be your supplier?

8. I know you have been considering this model for a long time. Just suppose we could meet your need for lower payments. Would there be any other reason why you would not get one today?

9. *If we were lower*, would you buy right now?

10. If this problem did not exist, would you sign the order at this time?

11. Is this the only problem that is holding you back?

12. If we can solve this problem right now, will you buy it now?

13. Is this the only concern you have about this purchase?

14. Obviously you have been thinking long and hard about this. What other concerns do you have?

15. Before I answer your question, are there any other concerns that are holding you back from enjoying this product?

16. Besides _____, what else are you concerned with?

17. I am glad you brought that up. Is that your most important concern?

18. Is there anything else besides _____ that would prevent you from buying this?

19. Are you saying that if we can find a way to meet your needs for a lower down payment, we have a deal?

20. Are you saying that if we get you a maintenance agreement that includes the costs for parts, we have a deal?

21. _____

_____

_____

22. _____

_____

_____

Understanding Reasons Behind the Objection

1. I am surprised to hear you say that. What do you mean by "too high"?

2. Obviously you must have a reason for saying that. Would you mind if I asked what it is?

3. That's an interesting point. What makes you say that?

4. What do you mean by "too complicated"?

5. Could you tell me the reasons for and against making a decision at this time?

6. What seems to be the reason behind your plant manager's rejecting our specifications?

7.   Could you explain why your expansion plans have been put on hold?

8.   You obviously feel very strongly about that. What triggers such a strong reaction?

9.   Of course, you want to talk this over with your partner. *What items will you be discussing with him?*

10.   *I understand that this is a difficult decision for you.* What are some of the reasons that speak for and against buying this model?

11.   Would you mind explaining to me why you feel that way?

12.   *Is there something that is not being expressed here?* Why do I get the feeling that you are not as enthusiastic about this product as you have been?

13. Would you mind explaining to me why your colleague feels that way?

14. You have been very quiet. *Would you mind telling me what you are thinking about?*

15. *You don't seem to have as much urgency on this project as you had before.* Could you tell me what happened between our last visit and now?

16. Suppose we could find a way to get around the financing question. Would there be any reason against going ahead with this purchase?

17. I understand that you need more time to think. I'd like to help you. *What exactly do you need to think about?*

18. That is an interesting point. Why do you bring that up?

19. I very rarely have someone ask about that. What made you bring that up?

20. _____

_____

_____

21. _____

_____

_____

Answering Objections with Questions

1. Would you agree that it takes information, not time, to make a decision? *What kind of information are you really looking for to make a good decision?*

2. You know, the rotary telephone looked complicated to people who never owned a telephone before. Is it possible that our product only looks complicated to you?

3. I agree. Our price is a little higher, but so is our quality. Are you interested in saving $1,200 a year on maintenance?

4. Sure, it costs a little more. However, you have the assurance that it will cost much less over its lifetime. Isn't that the way your own products are made?

5. Would you agree that the quality of a product is remembered much longer than the price?

6. Would you agree that the sweetness of low price is quickly forgotten when you have to deal every day with the bitterness of low quality?

7. You and I know that the true price of this machine is determined by the amount of production work you can get out of it. Wouldn't you agree with that?

8. That brings up a question. Is low price more important than the life of the product?

9. That brings up a question. What is more important to you—to save a few hundred dollars now on a lower price, or to save a few thousand dollars over the lifetime of this high-quality product?

10. I understand how you feel about price, but would you tell me how you feel about our quality?

11. That brings up a question. How important is it to you to have a reliable machine and a reliable dealer standing behind that product on the rare occasions when you do need service?

12. Your point is well taken. It does cost more than any other product on the market. But why do you think we sell millions of them at these very same prices?

13. I appreciate how you feel. Many of my customers have made similar comments prior to buying from me. However, they all asked themselves: *Can I afford not to have the best? Won't it cost me more in the long run?*

14. I personally feel that the *price is too low for what you are getting.* Do you think that all these satisfied owners would have bought from us if they had not checked out the incredible cost savings they get with this service? Would you like to talk to some of the people who were in a similar situation as you are now?

15. It looks expensive, but don't you think this is an advantage?

16. I understand that you want to take more time to think about this purchase. But, may I ask you a question? *What will change tomorrow? What will you gain by waiting?*

And what will you lose by not taking advantage of this opportunity?

17. Do you know the definition of a "procrastinator"? Someone who can't take "now" for an answer. Let me ask you a question: Is there any logical reason you could not say yes right now?

18. That brings up a question. What are the advantages of waiting, and *what are the advantages of buying right now*?

19. Imagine what this product could do if you had it right now. Think of the time savings. Think of the increased productivity. Think of the pride of ownership. Think of the happy faces on your employees. Would you want to say no to them, just because of a little hesitation about the down payment?

20. Aren't you exaggerating a little bit? Aren't you saying that you deserve the very best after the many years of hard work you have been putting into this business?

21. _____

_____

_____

22. _____

_____

_____

CHAPTER 6

Closing Questions

The only sale you close is the one you get in response to your closing question. Everything else is order-taking, or mere conversation.

- Alternative Closes
- Assumptive Closes
- Summary Closes
- Extra Incentive Closes
- Impending Event Closes
- Conditional Closes
- Direct Closes
- "Yes-Set" Closes

(Note: For "Trial Closes," see Chapter 4, "Presentation Questions.")

Alternative Closes

1.   Shall we handle the paperwork at *your office* or *mine*?

2.   Would you want to start *this week* or *next week*?

3.   Do you want this in *red* or in *blue*?

4.   Would you like this shipped *by mail* or do you need it *overnight*?

5.   Do you prefer *cash* or *credit*?

6.   Would you want to have us ship *one dozen* or do you prefer *two dozen* so you won't have to pay twice for shipping?

7.   Would you like us to send you a *letter of agreement*, or would you prefer giving me your *purchase order*?

8. Would you be *financing this purchase* or do you prefer *getting the cash discount*?

9. Would you like to have your lawyer write *a new contract* or do you feel comfortable using *the same one we used the last time*?

10. Do you want *our truck to deliver it*, or *can your driver pick it up* so you save on shipping?

11. Would you need this before *the end of the month* or can you possibly wait until *the tenth of next month*?

12. Do you prefer the *automatic* or would you like the *manual controls*?

13. What would make you happier, the *extended warranty* or the *service contract*?

CHAPTER 6

14. Would you be comfortable with *installing it yourself* or would you like us to *send you our application specialist* for one day?

15. Are you thinking about getting the *larger* diameter, or do you want the *smaller* one?

16. Do you need the *plastic* model or would you want to have *wood*?

17. Would you like the *economy* or the *deluxe* model?

18. _____

_____

_____

19. _____

_____

_____

Assumptive Closes

1. *Isn't that an ideal fit?* You want high quality and high productivity, and we are the leading company in both areas, right?

2. *You seem to be in agreement with me.* Can we take care of the paperwork now?

3. *I think we are walking step-in-step.* What's the next thing we need to take care of before your comptroller can write the check?

4. I guess *we are in harmony* on all the major points, aren't we?

5. *I feel like I'm on the same side of the table as you are.* Don't you think we are partners in this now?

6. *We've been working shoulder-to-shoulder.* Isn't that what you expect when you get a better supplier?

7. *I get the feeling we have really created a win/win relationship here.* Haven't we? Shall we go ahead and formalize it?

8. *It is rare that I get to work so closely with the final decision maker*—all the way up to the completion of the deal. Don't you feel it was well worth the effort?

9. *We've covered the major points to your satisfaction,* haven't we?

10. *It looks like we've overcome all the negative thinking here.* All is well that ends well, wouldn't you agree?

11. Now that this final point is cleared up, *we finally have a common purpose*. Aren't you excited about getting this new model?

12. *It's settled then*: The only way to solve the productivity problem is to get this new product, correct?

13. Since you have seen for yourself that this new model will meet your specifications, may I assume that *you would like me to reserve one for you*?

14. *Aren't you pleased that you came to the same conclusion as Mr. Jones?* He has been enjoying having this product now for over two years. How much money will this product make you over the next two years?

15. *You seem to understand this point very well. What can we do to speed up the purchasing process so we can get you the early delivery you wanted?*

16. _____

_____

_____

17. _____

_____

_____

Summary Closes

1.   (Customer's name), you have seen the cost-saving features of this proposal. *You know that this will improve your operation in several ways:* more speed, more accuracy, and lower cost. When would you like us to put this plan into operation?

2.   You have seen how our shipment plan will meet your deadline, and since you insist, we will extend the warranty by six months and you will get the extra 2 percent discount. Doesn't that give you just about everything you wanted? Congratulations! You are a tough negotiator!

3.   Mrs._____, since we agree that our delivery date is satisfactory, our terms competitive, and we seem to have overcome the financing hurdle, would you please initial this agreement?

4. Since we agree that time is your major concern and since we have satisfied your requirements in terms of delivery and price, *may I phone in the order now?*

5. May I take a moment to summarize the major benefits you will get with this plan? First, the performance guarantee; second, the extended warranty; third, the low-interest financing; and fourth, this product will get you the security and comfort you always wanted. Isn't that worth celebrating? Shall we take care of the paperwork and then celebrate?

6. Can we review for a moment why this is the best choice for you? First, you will have higher productivity. Second, it will save you

$75 per hour in service. And, third, you will have our three-year warranty. Doesn't that cover all of your needs?

7. Let's look at this decision from the benefit angle, okay? The first benefit you get is the higher trade-in value which means that you will have no down payment. The second benefit is that you will get our maintenance contract free for the first year, which will save you $450. The third benefit is that this machine will perform at a 17 percent higher production rate, which means that you will earn more money every single week. Aren't these three benefits enough reason for going ahead with this, or would you like me to go on?

8. Could you help me with writing the benefits of this product on this sheet of paper? Let's see—we have agreed that you like the quality. Then you seem to like the design features. Next we could add the financing plan and the low monthly payments. *Don't you think that these important benefits speak for going ahead with this now?*

9. What more could you ask for? You get the lower price; you get higher performance with this improved model; and, you get the installation free of charge! Can we shake hands on the deal? [Extend hand]

10. _____

_____

_____

11. _____

_____

_____

Extra Incentive Closes

1. If you order now, we will include a free two-day training program. Did you know that the value of this program is $450?

2. We are having a special promotion this week. If you sign up during this week, you will get a 5 percent discount. Isn't that enough of an incentive to go ahead?

3. For the next 10 days, this carries an additional discount of 7 percent. Are you prepared to pay the higher price later, or do you want to save by ordering now?

4. During this promotion, each purchase will include this beautiful display case. Isn't this a great offer?

5. For the next 30 days, we will provide the installation free of charge. Don't you think that will save you a lot of time and effort?

6. It's settled then. You want us to pay for the shipping and you'll absorb the warehouse cost?

7. It's okay then. We will give you the larger model at the same price and you will pay cash? That's a great deal, isn't it?

8. *Would you be interested in knowing about our special offer?* During this promotion, you can have two for one. Does that interest you?

9. This is your lucky day. Did you know that we have this model on special? Aren't you pleased?

10. *I can meet you more than halfway.* Did you know that when you order 10 you can pick two more free?

11. We would like to have you as a customer for a long time. *Shall we offer you an introductory discount of 10 percent on your first order?* Would that make your decision to go with us a little easier?

12. _____
_____
_____

13. _____
_____
_____

Impending Event Closes

1. Effective November 2, *there will be another price increase.* Would you like to save by ordering now?

2. Starting next month, our delivery schedule will increase by two weeks. Wouldn't you like to avoid having to wait?

3. This offer is only valid today. It's a terrific deal, isn't it?

4. These prices can't stay at that level for much longer. Did you know that two of our competitors already had a 5 percent increase? Can you risk waiting much longer?

5. I cannot guarantee that you will be able to buy this at the same price next week.

Do you know that the best time for saving money is right now?

6. Did I mention that this offer ends on the fifth? We already have the new price list. Would you like to know how much you will save by ordering today?

7. *If I were you, I would get one right now.* Did you know that we are almost sold out?

8. This is a very special opportunity. Did I tell you that there are only two models left? Would you believe that at the beginning of last week we had 50 in inventory?

9. This is our bestselling model. Did you know we cannot keep it in stock? We will be lucky if we get another shipment by the end of next month. Would you want me to put one aside for you?

10. Have you read the newspaper articles about the predicted shortages? If I were you, I would reserve a larger quantity today. Shall I write it up now?

11. You have probably heard the rumors about the shortages. They are true! We will get a price increase as early as next Wednesday. Would you like to save a few hundred dollars by ordering today?

12. _____

_____

_____

13. _____

_____

_____

Conditional Closes

1. *If we could meet your need for extended payments*, would you be willing to sign the order right now?

2. *If we extend our guarantee to include parts replacement*, will you go ahead with this order?

3. If we could meet your need for a higher trade-in allowance, would you make the commitment right now?

4. If we could provide you with the low-interest financing you had in mind, could we conclude the deal today?

5. If we lowered the price by 1 percent, would that be enough to finalize the transaction?

6. If I get my boss to approve these terms and conditions, will you go ahead with this today?

7. *If I can show you how this machine will be able to do the job you want and if I can guarantee the performance in writing,* do we have a deal?

8. If I can get it to you by Monday, do we have an agreement?

9. *If I can show you a way of financing this purchase without any negative effects on your cash flow,* will you buy one today?

10. If you can get the financing without paying the extra points, will you go ahead with this?

11. If we give you the extended warranty, will you order it?

12. If we can get you one at the old price, will you place an order now?

13. If your boss approves it, do we have *your* okay?

14. Let's assume that your wife will like it. Will you buy it?

15. If we can get it into our production schedule by next week, will you be interested in having us build one for you?

16. Are you saying that if we agree to delay the billing for 60 days, we've got a deal?

17. Are you telling me that if we can meet your need for a better trade-in, we've got the order?

18. *It sounds like you have made up your mind.* If we can get you the *first* order at these unusually low terms, then you will order from us every month at our regular low prices?

19. Suppose I can get these figures approved by my sales manager. Will you buy it today?

20. *Imagine for a moment that I can get you the financing at these rates.* Do we have a deal?

21. Suppose my boss will throw in the extra cost for installation. Do we have a deal?

22. Suppose my manager will add the cost for ocean freight. Do we have your commitment?

23. Imagine that in my phone call to the head office your proposed terms are approved. Will you be able to give us a check today?

24. Suppose we pay for the training of your operator and pick up the tab for the shipping. Can we order one for you today?

25. Suppose I can clear up the misunderstanding about the last order. Will you put us back on your list of approved vendors?

26. Suppose I can find a way to get around the price problem. Will you give me an order today?

27. _____

_____

_____

28. _____

_____

_____

CHAPTER 6

Direct Closes

1. It's settled then. Can we get you signed up now?

2. Can we have your okay on this agreement?

3. Does this agreement meet with your approval?

4. Can you initial this confirmation?

5. We have met your conditions. Can we do business?

6. *Do we have an agreement?*

7. Can we start celebrating your purchase?

8. Is it all right if we used your name in a press release saying that you have made this purchase today?

9. Are you happy with having made the decision to buy? Can you please sign this form?

10. Could you take this pen and press firmly? There are four copies.

11. Isn't it a great relief to put an end to your search? Can you please sign right here?

12. Isn't it wonderful that you have found what you have been looking for? Would you please put your initials on this?

13. Aren't you glad you decided to take the bull by the horns and make a decision today? *May I have your autograph, please?*

14. Aren't you excited about getting this new? Would you please let me have your John Hancock right here?

15. Don't you feel good about getting this extra protection? Here is the document that spells out all the details. Will you please review this now?

16. *Can't you just see the smiles on your employees' faces when you tell them you just bought this new machine?* Now we only need your signature right there, okay?

17. Isn't this one of the best purchases you have made all year? Congratulations! Would you please make out the check to (Your Company's Name) to reserve your model today?

18. *Did you know that the model you are going to get is the most popular one we make?* Can we do the paperwork now?

19. May I write this up now?

20. May I have your order now?

21. May we send you one today?

22. Do you want us to deliver one first thing next week?

23. *Are we in agreement on this purchase now?*

24. May I call my boss to tell him that we've received your order?

25. Do you want to take this with you now?

26. I can see that you like it. Can we have it loaded in your car?

27. I don't suppose there is any reason why we can't write this up now. Wouldn't you agree?

28. Since you like it so much, I have only one question to ask: When would you like it installed?

29. _____

_____

_____

30. _____

_____

_____

"Yes-Set" Closes

1. Do you like the quality of the product?
[Yes]

Do you like the colors you have selected?
[Yes]

Can you get the financing?   [Yes]

Then it seems that we can go ahead with the agreement, right?

2. Are you satisfied with the performance data?   [Yes]

Do you like the warranty plan?   [Yes]

Does this delivery schedule sound okay to you?   [Yes]

Then we should go ahead and reserve one for you, right?

3. Do you feel comfortable with this horsepower?   [Yes]

Are you pleased with the way it looks?

[Yes]

Does your husband like it?   [Yes]

Can we write it up now?

4.   Do you like the fact that you will save $4,000 in maintenance costs each year?

[Yes]

Are you happy with the performance?

[Yes]

Can you afford the down payment?

[Yes]

Could you write us a deposit check while I fill out the order form?

5.   Is blue your favorite color for office machines?   [Yes]

Did you like the automatic features?

[Yes]

Are you comfortable with the three-year financing?   [Yes]

Would you like to have yours delivered by Monday?

6. Are you pleased with the size of this building?   [Yes]

Do you like the design?   [Yes]

Are you satisfied with the security system? [Yes]

Would you like us to start your lease next month?

7. Were you impressed by the demonstration? [Yes]

Did the product meet your expectations? [Yes]

Did it have the features you wanted? [Yes]

Do you like the terms of the service contract?   [Yes]

Would you want us to install this by Friday?

CHAPTER 6

8. Wasn't that a great trial run?   [Yes]

Did you like the extra power?   [Yes]

Did you like the performance under difficult conditions?   [Yes]

It sounds like you want this one—right?

9. Do you enjoy having the best?   [Yes]

Do you have a preference for the larger model?   [Yes]

Are you comfortable with payments of $_____ per month?   [Yes]

Congratulations, you've just bought a new_____!

10. Is this the type of service contract you were looking for?   [Yes]

Are you satisfied with the speed?   [Yes]

Does the extra storage capacity meet your needs?   [Yes]

Shall we get the paperwork out of the way now?

_11._ Can you get by with 80-pound blue stock? [Yes]

Can you live with the delivery schedule? [Yes]

Can your accountant clear up the old balance by Monday?   [Yes]

Congratulations, we've got a deal!

_12._ Are you sure that the 120-horsepower model is strong enough for your application? [Yes]

Do you like the easily accessible controls? [Yes]

Are you happy with the quality and workmanship?   [Yes]

Can we write this up now?

13. _____

_____

_____

14. _____

_____

_____

CHAPTER 7

Upselling Questions

The best customers in the world are your existing customers. What do you think it would take to sell them more? A good question...

- Upselling Questions

Upselling Questions

1. And what else are you going to order today?

2. (Customer's name), you buy 300 _____ from us each month. If you also ordered 50 _____ along with that, I could give you a significant discount. Are you interested?

3. (Customer's name), you buy 40 _____ from us each week. If you increase that to more than 50, I could save you an additional 10 percent. Would you be interested in saving your company 10 percent more in this area?

4. (Customer's name), we are ready to unveil our whole new product line. We have been keeping it top secret until now. I want you to be among the very first few people to learn about it. When can we meet?

5. *If we were giving away, free of charge, any other product from our catalog, which product would you most want?*

6. *If your company had a larger budget, what would be the next product of ours you would have them buy?* Good, so you really do need that! Would you be interested in my showing you how you can afford it?

7. If you could afford it, what is the next thing you would buy from us?

8. I am puzzled. Why haven't you ordered more from us?

9. I am confused. You say you are happy with our products and services. Why haven't you made another purchase?

10. *Most of our customers place an order every three months.* Why is it we haven't seen your second order yet?

11. *Most of our clients plan one year in advance.* Would you like to place an order for next year if I guarantee you I can freeze in today's low prices?

12. Are you really happy with our _____? Then why haven't you bought more of it?

13. Did you know that our _____ comes in five other colors? Which other colors would you like in your next order?

14. Did you know that we now offer low-interest financing? You may want to take advantage of it by placing an order today. I don't know how much longer it will last.

You wouldn't want to miss this opportunity, would you?

15. Did you know that we have added four new models to our product line since you made your last purchase? When can you come in and take a look at them?

16. Did you know that we just added three new services to our payroll and accounting package? Can I tell you about them?

17. (Customer's name), *I haven't seen you in some time.* Can we set up a meeting and get together so that I can tell you about the terrific new products and services we are offering? When?

18. (Customer's name), I have been thinking about you and your company. We have made a lot of improvements and additions to our product line that I think could really benefit your company. When can we get together to talk about them?

19. (Customer's name), I read in the newspaper how your company has grown and expanded. I know you bought some of our smaller machines a few years ago. Do you think you are now ready to take a serious look at some of our more powerful units?

20. (Customer's name), did you see the new product announcements in all the trade newspapers about our _____? We are the talk of the industry! Would you like to know what everyone is talking about? When can we get together?

21. (Customer's name), we estimate that the useful life of our XYZ Fire Extinguisher is three years. I see from our records that your units are almost three years old now. Can we get together so that I can show you some of the latest fire prevention and fire extinguishing technology?

22. We are a completely different company now. We are under new management. Shouldn't you examine our new products?

23. We are a totally new company now. You really owe it to yourself to take a fresh new look at our products and services, don't you?

24. *We have bought another company* and have added some spectacular new products and services. When can we get together so that I can show you what we now offer?

25. (Customer's name), we are now making a service available to our smaller clients that was previously offered only to the largest, most powerful companies. Would you be interested in taking a look at it?

26. (Customer's name), we are introducing a powerful new machine. I am convinced it will give you a tremendous edge over the competition. When can I show it to you?

27. What needs do you have that we have not yet addressed?

28. What problems does your company still have in production?

29. (Customer's name), our company offers over 1,000 different products. Out of that huge range of products, I am sure there are many that you could use. Which ones most interest you?

30. (Customer's name), you are only using one of our many, many different services. Why is that?

31. If we could add any additional products to our catalog, what would you like to see in the future?

32. You have been a very good customer of ours and we appreciate that. That's why we'd like to offer you a special 10 percent discount on another product of ours. Of all of our other products, which one is of greatest interest to you?

33. (Customer's name), I know you buy 100 _____ from us and 100 from our competition. If we could have all your business, I could extend to you a 7 percent discount. Do you think your boss would go for this?

34. Why aren't we doing more business together?

35. What do we have to do to get more of your business?

36. Why aren't you buying more from us?

37. Many of our clients started small with us. *Why do you think they started giving us more and more of their business?*

38. Why have your orders to us decreased in size? Have we let you down in any way?

39. Some of our very biggest clients were at one time small clients. Would you like to learn what they learned?

40. *Why have your orders to us decreased in frequency?* Is there some way we can get them back up to the old levels?

41. Why have you started to give other companies some of the business you used to give us? Is there something we can do to win back your business? What?

42. Are you totally pleased with our products and services? Good! Does that mean you would like to increase your orders with us?

43. _____
_____
_____

44. _____
_____
_____

CHAPTER 8

Referral Questions

Closing a sale can feed you for a week. Asking for referrals after every close can feed you for a lifetime.

- Referral Questions

Referral Questions

1. Did you know that the average person has 200 friends and close acquaintances? It is true! *Of the 200 people closest to you, who do you think would be most interested in learning about our products and services?*

2. I was wondering if you could help me with this. *Would you be able to give me the names of two of your colleagues whom you think would be excited to learn about this product?*

3. How many people can you think of who might be interested in using a system like this?

4. Who else do you know who might be interested in improving their company's productivity?

5. I am sure someone like you must have many friends. Who else do you know who is interested in owning the very best?

6. You have told me you are very happy with our product (service). Is there any reason you wouldn't want two of your friends to enjoy the same benefits you have enjoyed? Who should I call on?

7. Most of our customers give us between two and five leads to new prospects. How many could you give us? Who are they?

8. Our average customer gives us three leads to new prospects. Could you give us more or less than the average? Who are they?

9. You have given me the name of _____ as a lead. May I use your name when I call him?

10. You have given me the name of _____ as a lead. Do you suggest I call him or drop in to see him?

11. Thanks for the referral. Do you suggest I call him or send him a letter?

12. Thanks for the lead. How long have you known her?

13. Thank you for the referral. *Has he ever bought a product or service like ours in the past?* When? What did he buy?

14. Thank you for the referral. Does he have the authority to buy our product (service)?

Is there anyone else there I should talk to? Who?

15. Thank you for the referral. *Would you mind calling him to let him know I will be in touch?*

16. Thank you for the recommendation. Could I ask you a favor? Would you please call him and set up a meeting for us?

17. Thank you for the lead. May I ask you a favor? *Would you please come with me my first visit with him?*

18. Do you belong to any professional groups whose members might be interested in our products (services)?

19. *Do you belong to any social groups where I might speak about our products (services)?* Which groups?

20. Would any of your relatives be interested in our products (services)? Who?

21. Would any of your friends be interested in our products (services?) Who?

22. Would any of your coworkers be interested in our investments? Who?

23. Would any of your children be interested in our educational programs? Which ones?

24. Would any of your neighbors be interested in our programs? Who?

25. Is there any reason you wouldn't want to give us some referrals?

26. *I know you were sincere when you complimented us about our products.*

Who else do you know who would be interested in our high-quality products?

27. Did you know that most of our business comes from referrals? It does! Who can you refer me to?

28. Did you know that I was referred to you by _____? Yes, and I am grateful to him for the referral. Now, who can you refer me to?

29. I know you are not a hermit. I know you are a popular person. How many of your friends would benefit from this opportunity?

30. I know you are a highly respected person in your field. A referral from you could really help me out. Who could you introduce me to as a lead or referral?

31. It will just take a minute for you to jot down the names and phone numbers of a couple of your friends who might be interested in our products or services. Would you mind doing that?

32. You don't know anyone who would be interested in our products or services? Not anyone? How can you say that?

33. _____
_____
_____

34. _____
_____
_____

CHAPTER
9

Follow-up
Questions

Do you give up or clean up or follow up?

- Level of Satisfaction
- Product Performance
- Service/Maintenance

Level of Satisfaction

1. I would be interested to know *how your new machine is working out.* Are you happy with it?

2. Could you tell me *in which ways this product has met your needs*?

3. Were you *satisfied with the delivery*?

4. How do you feel about the way our installation crew handled the job?

5. Are you still pleased with your decision to get the larger model?

6. Are you glad you got the extended warranty protection?

7. Do your people seem well satisfied with the product?

8. Would you be able to tell me some of the reactions from your management to this new product?

9. Is the product (service) making your life easier?

10. What do your neighbors think of it?

11. Do your kids use it? How often?

12. Does your spouse like it?

13. How have you been using this product?

14. Could you tell me what happened on the day you received the shipment?

15. Since you now know the product well, how would you sell it if you were me?

16. Are you happy with the fact that you own the highest quality system?

17. _____

_____

_____

18. _____

_____

_____

Product Performance

1. Now that you have been using our product for _____ weeks, could you tell me more about your production figures?

2. I was wondering, how much has your productivity gone up as a result of getting this machine?

3. Would you be able to tell me specifically in which ways the new product has helped you reduce operating costs?

4. Have you noticed a decrease in your maintenance bills?

5. Have you been able to measure the differences in productivity between the old model and the new one?

6. Have you seen an improvement in your sales yet?

7. In what ways is this model making your life easier?

8. How does our product compare to the competition's model that you had been using?

9. Could you share some performance data with me?

10. Is our product as effective as you thought it would be?

11. Now that you have had the opportunity to measure the production, did our machine fulfill all of your requirements?

12. Would you like to share with me how you have been using the product? May I help you with suggestions on how to make your job even easier?

13. Would you mind writing us a short note about your performance data? This would help us a great deal in making this product available to other customers who are in a similar situation.

14. Have you told other people about how well this product is performing for you? What were their reactions? Would some of them be interested in a demonstration?

15. Doctor, how has this drug been working for your patients? Do you think it has an even wider range of uses than we initially discussed?

16. _____

_____

_____

17. _____

_____

_____

_____

Service/Maintenance

1. Have you been keeping track of your maintenance costs?

2. Is the service manual easy enough for your people to read and understand?

3. Have you heard any comments about the serviceability of the machine?

4. Could we go over your maintenance records? I'd like to figure out how I can help you save money in this area.

5. Are you happy with the way our service department handled your recent problem?

6. Are you happy with the fuel consumption?

7. Do you think that the automatic model has cut your operating costs? How much?

8. Do you know that we have a new service hotline? May I ask you to put these stickers with the new number on it on all of our products?

9. Now that you have had this machine for some time, have you been able to figure out the savings in repair bills?

10. You seem to be pleased with the trouble-free operation. Could you give us a letter of reference mentioning this fact? I certainly would appreciate that.

11. May we talk to your mechanic to review your needs for extra parts?

12. Are you running low on any service supplies?

13. Have you been ordering our original parts? Did you get prompt delivery?

14. *Is there anything in the service area we need to improve?*

15. You know that a machine is only as good as the company that stands behind it. *How would you rate our performance in the service, parts, and maintenance areas?*

16. *Is there anything I can do to help you with your plans for service?*

17. Have our trainers been helpful? Have they met your expectations?

18. Has the insurance claims department handled your claims promptly? Is there anything more they can do or I can do to serve you better?

19. _____
_____
_____

20. _____
_____
_____

CHAPTER 10

Tested Questioning Techniques

The Apology Question

The purpose of this question is to appease the customer's hostile or noncooperative attitude. Your visible reluctance in asking the question will lower tension in the relationship. (Do not overuse this question.)

1. Look, I have probably come to the wrong person, but who in your company is responsible for purchasing cleaning supplies?

2. I am absolutely lost. Could you explain your purchasing procedure one more time?

3. I am sorry, but you lost me at the last traffic light. Could you go over the directions one more time?

4. I'm sorry I didn't make the features and benefits of our product clear to you. *What did I neglect to explain?*

5. I apologize if I seem forward, but could you tell me why you haven't done business with our company in the past?

6. I hope this isn't confidential information, but could you tell me the chemical-cleaning formula you use now?

7. I must be kind of slow today. I'm sorry. Could you explain to me again your reasons for putting off this decision?

8. I am sorry if I am taking up too much of your time. *When can we meet again so that I can more fully explain the details of our system?*

9. May I ask a favor of you? I hate to inconvenience you, but I'd be very grateful if you would go along with me when I see your boss. Is that possible?

10. I hope you don't think I'm too forward, but I'd really appreciate a referral from you. Who else do you know who might benefit from our payroll services?

11. I hope I am not imposing on you, but could you answer a few questions for me to help me prepare *the best proposal possible*?

The Benefit Question

The purpose of this technique is to build your customer's interest in your product or services by focusing on the areas that are of *most interest to him or her*.

1. Could you tell me what benefits you think this feature will bring you?

2. How will you benefit from working with a large company?

3. Do you see any benefit in having more easily accessible controls?

4. Do you see the value in having the most advanced engineering available?

5. Are you more interested in our *lower price* or in our *extra* features?

6. Have you thought about the *status* and *prestige* you will enjoy from having the very best?

7. What is it worth to you to be admired by all of those around you?

8. What is an ironclad guarantee worth to you?

9. Is being able to save over $1,000 during our sale of interest to you?

10. How valuable is a money-back guarantee to you?

11. Is it important to you to have the best extended warranty in the business?

12. Would you like to own the most accurate and realistic audio system available in the world today?

13. *Would you be interested in a medically supervised diet and exercise system that is guaranteed to take off 20 pounds and keep it off?*

CHAPTER 10

The Checklist Question

This question triggers your customer to give you a *complete, item-by-item response* as to what he or she wants or needs.

1. Would you be able to tell me exactly what specific criteria you are looking for?

2. What items are on your shopping list today?

3. Could you describe the type of features you had in mind?

4. What are the most essential points we need to consider?

5. What does your "wish list" look like?

6. Tell me about your dream vacation, okay?

7. When you and your wife talked about this purchase, *what were the criteria that kept coming up?*

8. In order of priority, which features and benefits are most important to you?

9. How, exactly, do you know that all of your requirements have been met?

10. *On a scale of 1 to 10*, let's rank the importance of each of these criteria.

11. Is there anything at all we left off your list of criteria?

12. Are you sure there is nothing else you are looking for in a machine like this?

13. Is anything else important to you in selecting a bank? What, specifically?

The Common Grounds Question

Your question will suggest similarities and common viewpoints that you and your customer share, thus strengthening your personal as well as your business relationship.

1. You and I know that this is a better-quality product, but how are we going to convince your finance department?

2. Isn't this an ideal fit? You want high quality and high productivity, and we are the leading company in both areas, aren't we?

3. You and I both have similar backgrounds in this industry. *Are we seeing eye-to-eye as to which product best fits your needs?*

4. We've been working on this shoulder-to-shoulder. That's a good feeling, isn't it?

5. It is rare that I get to work as closely with a customer as I've had the opportunity to work with you. I've enjoyed the relationship. Do you think you've gotten a lot out of it?

6. We've established a lot of common ground, don't you think? What's the next thing we need to do to get this deal approved?

7. Well, it looks like it is you and me against the negative thinkers. What do we need to do to push this through to approval?

8. You told me that you really want to buy this machine to begin enjoying its benefits. I'd like to sell it to you. So we have a common goal and purpose. How can we overcome the roadblocks that are in our way and that prevent us from reaching our common goal?

9. You and I both detest that simplistic rah-rah-rah old-fashioned sales training. Would you be interested in learning about a sales training system that is based on studies of more than 200 of the top sales forces in America?

10. I see you work as late as I do. What do you say I pick you up tonight at seven, and we can talk about this deal over dinner. Okay?

The Comparison Question

This technique is designed to help the customer recognize the differences between all the products on the market, and *to appreciate the special benefits your products offer.*

1. How do you rate the new system compared to the one you installed last year?

2. Where do you see the differences between these two models?

3. Where do you find similarities and where do you see differences in these two machines?

4. Is there anything you think that model has that our model doesn't have?

5. Are you interested in the *less expensive system* or the *more elaborate one?*

6. Did you know that products in this field range in price from $_____ to $_____? Which price range best fits your budget?

7. It's a fact that bank interest rates range from 9 to 14 percent. Did you know that? What interest rate were you planning to pay?

8. Would you be interested in a more expensive or a less expensive model than the one you last purchased? Why?

9. *How do you rate these three models?*

10. Without regard to price, which model do you think is superior?

11. Do you really see any differences between all the products competing for your attention in this field? May I show you why our product is the bestselling brand?

12. What will you need to find out to decide that our product is the finest of all the ones available?

13. *What other brands and models have you looked at?*

The Compliment Question

Paying a sincere compliment will *never* displease a customer. Beware of insincere flattery because it will backfire. If you look for something to like or compliment in a customer, you will find it!

1. You must have a lot of willpower. How were you able to stop smoking cold turkey?

2. If you don't mind my asking, what is your secret for staying so well informed?

3. Could you tell me how you manage to keep your calm under these trying conditions?

4. I love the way your office is furnished. Who is your decorator?

5. You've done a great job of remodeling this building. How did you do it?

6. Is that your car outside? It's a classic!

7. Is that a picture of your family? What a great-looking family!

8. I just heard about your new product introductions. How do you always manage to stay two years ahead of the competition?

9. I see your company just won another award. Congratulations on a job well done! How do you manage to do it year after year?

10. Are you still on the company softball team? I've heard you've got the fastest arm in the West! Is that true?

11. Is that your golfing trophy? What did you shoot to win it?

12. I've heard you are a great chef. Where did you learn to cook so well?

The Conditional Question

With this type of question, you are offering an incentive in exchange for a positive answer.

1. If I knew your criteria for evaluating this type of product, I could give you more details. Could you share some of these with me now?

2. If I could share three good reasons with you why this product will outperform any other on the market, would you be willing to agree to a demonstration?

3. If I could show you a simple idea that would save you an extra $400 in operating costs every month, would you be willing to consider this proposal?

4.   If I could show you a method of payment that would create a positive cash flow so that your purchase will be 100 percent self-financed, would you be interested?

5.   If I could show you a way of reducing staff turnover by 10 percent this year, would you consider using our executive placement services?

6.   If I could give you a trade-in credit of $10,000 for your car, would you make the commitment to purchase this new Cadillac?

7.   If we could provide you with below-market financing, could we do the deal?

8.   If I were willing to drive out to see you, would you give me a full hour of your time with no interruptions?

9. It I offered to take you out to lunch at the restaurant of your choice, could I have your undivided attention for two hours?

10. I know you are very busy, but if I were willing to meet with you at 6:30 a.m., could we do it?

11. If I could show you a set of negotiating techniques that would give you an upper hand over the union, would you consider putting me on retainer at your corporation?

The Confidential Question

This questioning technique is designed to establish an atmosphere of confidentiality between you and your prospect. This technique will often result in more candid responses than you would get through direct questioning.

1. Strictly off the record, how many competitive models did you look at?

2. Just between friends, what are your plans for next year?

3. Just between us, how much discount did they offer you?

4. May I ask you a question off the record? [Yes] What is your procedure for purchasing this type of service?

5. May I ask you an honest question? How much did you pay for this?

6. Confidentially, is your purchasing manager able to understand the way this offer is written?

7. *Just between us*—what was seen as our greatest strength? Our greatest weakness? What can we do to correct that weakness?

8. Totally off the record—is there any way of getting that other company out? Is there anything at all you are dissatisfied with? What?

9. *May I ask you a confidential question?* How much did you budget for this?

10. *May I ask you a confidential question?* Was our price higher or lower than you expected? By how much?

11. *Just between you and me*—is there anything, anything at all, we could do at this time to increase our odds of getting the order? What?

12. I promise you I'll only use this number once, and he'll never know who gave it to me. What is the president's number?

13. *Just between the two of us*—is there anyone else here in the club who needs these kinds of services? Who?

The Confirmation Question

This question can protect you from misunderstandings, and it is often used prior to a closing question.

1. It's settled then that we will pay for the shipping and you will absorb the warehouse cost?

2. You're saying that you will go ahead if your wife gives her okay, correct? Let's call her now!

3. Let me ask you one more time, just to be sure: Your truck could pick up the shipment on Monday at 8 a.m.?

4. So, we're agreed: It's the blue metallic, with leather seats and a sunroof?

5. Does this mean you're most interested in the 512K model with the dual disk drives and a laser printer?

6. Are you saying that you'll agree to the purchase if we delay billing you for 90 days?

7. So, you'd like 100 units if we can get the lower price or 50 units at the other price?

8. Do I understand you that if we could close escrow in 30 days, guaranteed, you'll want to go ahead?

9. So, you do want it shipped by UPS rather than Express Mail?

10. If we can get you 12 percent financing, then you are interested?

11. We are in agreement then on model, price, delivery, and the service contract, correct? Is there anything else?

12. What you are saying is that you will trade in your old model if we can get you a new one at the price of $_____. Is that right?

The Definition Question

To get the complete story and to avoid misunderstanding, ask customers to define exactly what they mean. Definition questions clarify statements, comments, issues, trends, and priorities.

1. Could you give me an example of what you mean?

2. How long would you like this "extended" escrow to be?

3. How long would you like this "extended" warranty to go?

4. How would you like to measure the "effectiveness" of the training?

5. I was wondering if you could fill me in on what you mean by "too complicated"?

6. You told me that you wanted to save 15 percent. Do you mean gross or net?

7. "Better" in what way?

8. How do you measure productivity?

9. What exactly do you mean by a "low interest rate"?

10. When you say you want a house with a view, how far up the hill do you want to be?

11. What do you mean when you say you want a dog that's "easy to house-train"?

12. You said you were interested in a "large" disk drive. How much storage space do you think you'll need?

13. You said you are only willing to take a vacation in a "safe" part of the world. What do you mean by "safe"? What areas do you consider "safe"?

14. I remember your talking about your budget being "limited." What exactly do you mean by "limited"?

The Expectation Question

Knowing your customer's type and level of expectation will help you tailor your presentation to his or her needs.

1. What are your expectations of this product?

2. What problems do you definitely want to avoid?

3. When would you like it delivered?

4. What exactly do you expect us to do in this situation?

5. What color were you hoping to get it in?

6. How could we make you a customer for life?

7. Were you planning to go with the regular warranty or the extended warranty?

8. How many bedrooms and bathrooms did you want?

9. How much land did you want?

10. What rate of return were you expecting?

11. Which options and extras were you planning to buy with this?

12. How many hours a week were you planning to use this machine?

13. How many years do you plan to keep this furniture?

14. Were you expecting to make this decision by yourself or with someone else? Who?

15. Were you expecting to look very much longer before making up your mind? How much longer?

The Experience Question

Customers love to share their experiences with you. This technique reveals your personal interest in them and their needs. It also gives them a chance to show you their hot buttons. When you know what someone has responded to in the past, you have a very good idea of what he or she will like today.

1. You are an expert on the inner workings of your company. I realize that you don't have any budget for an expenditure of this type. But, is there any other budget we can utilize? Which budget still has some unspent money in it? Who do we need to talk to get approval to use it? Thank you! I value your help!

2. You have bought these items many times in the past. What has been your experience in terms of quantities ordered? Should you order _____ boxes per month or _____ boxes per week?

3. What is your experience in dealing with your boss? Is he or she likely to go for this? Why or why not?

4. In terms of your past experience, what did you like most about products in this field? How can we provide you with more of that?

5. I trust and value your opinion. Does your company see this service as a necessity or as a luxury? How can we get them to see this service as a necessity?

6. I value your judgment. How much time do you suggest I take in explaining our products to your supervisor? Does he or she like brief meetings or longer, more detailed explanations?

7. I know you are the most knowledgeable person I could ask this question of. What is holding up the purchase decision? Is it price? Is it service? Is it delivery? Is it our warranty? [Keep asking until the customer tell you what it is, then satisfy them on that point.]

8. You are obviously very experienced in this area. What would you do if you were in my position? How could we get the business?

9. Your company has dealt with many suppliers in this field. You have stopped doing business with a number of them. I value your opinion. What went wrong in those relationships? How can we avoid such problems?

The Explanation Question

It is important to ask explanation questions with an attitude of caring and genuine interest. Your attitude will determine whether your prospects will trust you enough to share their buying motives with you.

1. I feel like a professional interviewer with you. I hope you don't mind all these questions. It will help me to meet your needs if I know more about what they are. What do you see as your number-one need? Why? Your number-two need? Why?

2. I know you are doing business with three companies in this field. Would you mind sharing with me what we could do to increase the percentage of business you give us?

3. Would you mind explaining to me why you feel that way? Would you mind explaining to me why your associate feels that way?

4. You impress me as an astute observer. What was his reaction when you told him the price?

5. You really know how to work well with a sales representative. Can you tell me what I can do to help you in your job?

6. You don't seem to care very much about that. Why is that so? Many of our customers think that is one of the most important benefits. Are you saying it is not important to you?

7. We have looked at the logical reasons behind that decision. Can you share with me some the emotional reasons? Who else will be using this? How will they feel about it?

8. You have shared with me the emotional reasons behind this decision. What are the logical reasons? What sort of return on investment will you be looking for?

9. It seems like something is not being said. What haven't you told me about yet?

10. We very seldom lose business. Would you mind sharing with me why we lost your business? What can we do to regain it?

The Fact-Finding Question

There are millions of facts you can ask for. Don't just randomly collect facts. You will be overwhelmed with trivia. Be a gourmet when gathering facts. The facts you want to hear are those that can lead you to the sale.

1. Who is responsible for making this decision?

2. When did you start in this position?

3. Where is your West Coast office?

4. Why do you think you need this model and not some other model?

5. How long will it take to make this purchase decision? Is there anything we can do to speed up the process? What?

6. How many people are working in Plant B?

7. Do you have a lot of experience in making purchases of this type? How do you like to make these purchases?

8. Are you planning to trade something in for this? What? How long have you had it? What kind of trade-in price are you looking for?

9. What other divisions of your company might be interested in our products and services? Who should I contact there? What is the phone number?

10. Is there anything I have neglected to ask you about? What?

11. Is there anything you haven't told me about? What?

The Feeling Question

The feeling question explores your customer's personal reactions to your product or service. It goes beyond the purely factual to look at his or her complete range of emotions. Feeling questions show you care about your prospect as an individual. These are excellent questions for building rapport.

1. I understand how you feel. What do you think will result from this?

2. You seem pleased. Is there anything I can do to make you even happier?

3. I sense that you are a little hesitant about this. Why is that?

4. You look really concerned. What thoughts do you have on this?

5. I sense that you are unsure here. Why is that?

6. You seem much happier than usual. What's the cause for celebration?

7. How do you feel about this new finance plan?

8. You seem to be holding something back. What is it?

9. I can't quite read you on that one. How does it appeal to you?

10. How do you feel about our new price increase? I'd like to know your true feelings.

11. What is your real concern? What is your real feeling about this?

12. In your heart of hearts, do you think we have your business?

13. You look sad. Did we do something to disappoint you? What? How can we make up for it?

14. You seem very, very pleased with our products. Would you mind sharing that excitement in a letter to my boss? Thank you!

15. You seem rushed. Why? Should we meet some other time? When?

16. Are you comfortable here? If not, where should we meet? At my office? At a restaurant?

The Future Prediction Question

This type of question identifies the customer's future plans so you can build your long-term selling strategy. The information you gather from these questions will help you prepare for any eventuality.

1. How long do you think this will last you?

2. Where do you see yourself in the company hierarchy five years from now?

3. Where would you like to be three years from now? How do you plan to get there?

4. If you could keep this same low price, would you consider weekly purchases and delivery instead of monthly? Wouldn't that save on your warehouse space?

5. Do you plan to hire anyone else next year? How will you train them?

6. Do you plan to expand to any new geographical areas? Where? When are you planning this expansion?

7. A lot of companies are planning cutbacks. Is this true of your company? When? What form will these cutbacks take? How will this affect your purchasing plans?

8. Could we still have the order if we couldn't get it for you in that color?

9. When do you plan to retire? What kind of legacy do you want to leave?

10. How do you want to be remembered after you are gone?

11. How are you preparing for the future?

12. How will you meet the new competitive demands in this industry?

13. What do you plan to do when other companies copy your products?

14. Some of your products have been on the market for a long time. When they become dated, what do you plan to do?

The "Good Reason" Question

This question puts the ball in the customer's court. If he or she cannot come up with a good reason not to buy, he or she will feel much more impelled to make a positive decision to buy.

1. Can you give me one good reason not to buy this machine?

2. Is there any justification for not increasing the size of your order?

3. Do you know any person who wouldn't go for a deal like this?

4. Is there any good reason to put this off any longer?

5. Do you need any other good reasons to buy our services? What?

6. Is there any good reason to deny yourself the pleasure of owning the very best?

7. Is there any reason you should pay a higher price?

8. Can you give me even one reason for not taking advantage of this special low interest rate?

9. Isn't that one more reason not to put this important decision off any longer?

10. Do you know of any reason your boss would not approve this order?

11. Is there any reason to finance this when you could easily pay cash?

12. Are there any good reasons I should not talk to your boss?

13. Do you know of any reason why the director of purchasing would procrastinate on making this decision?

14. Can you give me three good reasons why you should put this off?

15. Is there any reason you have to have this machine in off-white rather than in glacier white?

The Hesitancy Question

You can make a stronger appeal for help and cooperation from customers by deliberately stalling before asking the complete question. This is like the "one-two" punch in boxing. Hesitating after the first part of the question makes customers more inclined to listen to the second part and to help you.

1. I may be confused but . . . aren't low price and high quality of interest to you?

2. I'm kind of slow today. [Pause] What did you mean when you said _____?

3. I am curious. [Pause] Why have you given the government half of your annual income instead of giving it to your family and loved ones?

4. I'm not the kind of person who likes to make guesses, so . . . what features and benefits are you most interested in?

5. I'm sorry, but I don't understand this. [Pause] Why haven't you automated this factory by now?

6. I don't know how to put this. [Pause] Isn't it time to offer some up-to-date sales skills training for your salespeople?

7. This is a delicate issue, but ... have you thought of totally throwing out your old computers and getting some new ones?

8. I have no idea if this appeals to you or not, but ... have you ever considered a first-class trip to China?

9. I may be dreaming, but ... don't you and your family really deserve to be living in this beautiful new three-story house?

10. Please correct me if I am wrong but … aren't you a man who always insists on the best?

11. I am perplexed. [Pause] Were you most concerned about speed or about image quality in selecting this computer printer?

12. Would you help me? [Pause] What would you do if you were in my position?

The Humorous Question

Appropriate humor relaxes your customer and makes him or her feel good. Humor can sometimes succeed where nothing else can. Humorous questions, when properly used, can sometimes accomplish what no amount of lecturing or product information can do. Plus, sales professionals who use a little humor tend to be remembered much longer than most other salespeople. Humorous questions can give your prospects and customers a fresh new perspective on you and your products!

1. Did you know that we accept cash with proper identification?

2. Are you trying to tell me you want high quality and a low price?

3. You don't mean to say you want a guarantee with this, do you?

4. Did you know that we usually require your first-born son as a down payment on a purchase like this?

5. Will you be able to provide us with 100 credit references?

6. Which do you want more—low quality or a high price?

7. Between the colors of light black, medium black, or dark black, which do you prefer?

8. You don't expect us to service this thing, do you?

9. Did I tell you I lied to you about the price?

10. Did I tell you we charge $45,000 for postage and handling?

11.   Oh, by the way, did you know that 99 percent of the price you pay is a commission to me?

12.   Did you know that this product is constructed entirely in Antarctica using only naturally occurring elements?

The Imagination Question

There are few forces in the universe more powerful than the human imagination. By tapping into the imagination of your projects and customers, you can get them to "mentally own" your products and services. Once they have "mentally owned" these products and services, it is but a small step to get them to own them in real life. Use imagination questions to trigger all the senses of your customers!

1. Can you imagine the positive impact this will have on your career here at the company?

2. Can you imagine that you will be the man (woman) who will go down in history for having finally automated this plant?

3. Can you imagine the expression on your husband's face when you give him this new Jet-Ski?

4. Imagine yourself impressing all your business colleagues in Europe with your new skills in the German language. Did you know we can have you fluent in conversational German in seven weeks?

5. Can you feel the wind blowing through your hair as you race down the freeway in your new convertible?

6. Imagine getting concert hall realism in your own home! Can you hear the flute over there? And the tympani drums over there? And the violins over there?

7. Can you imagine a higher quality product at a lower price?

8. Can you imagine what real estate will be worth in this beach community?

9. Can you see yourself floating on an inflatable raft in your new swimming pool on a hot summer day with a cool drink in your hand?

10. Can you imagine what a 10 percent reduction in raw materials cost will do for your bottom line?

The Importance Question

The purpose of this question is to determine the customer's values and priorities. Once you know these, you will know exactly what to sell. You won't waste your time describing or demonstrating products or features the customer is not interested in. Never guess what the prospect wants! Use importance questions to get the customer to give you the combination to the vault!

1. Would your boss place the same order of importance on these features and benefits as you have placed on them? Shall we check it out just to make sure?

2. Is it more important to you to get a lower interest rate today, perhaps with a slightly higher purchase price, or would you want the lowest possible price with a slightly higher interest rate?

3. Who in your company asked you to make price the most important buying criterion?

4. Your company's directions to vendors say that quality is most important. You seem to be implying that price is. Which is it, may I ask?

5. Is it more important to buy something that will impress your neighbors or something that will impress you?

6. Can you think of any reason why this benefit wouldn't be of prime importance to you?

7. In our last meeting, you said that the computer's multiuser capabilities were most important to you. Is that still your number-one criterion?

8. Which features and benefits are least important to you? Why?

9. Earlier, you said that this feature and that feature were both equally important to you. Now, we have examined both of them in much greater detail. Which one could you now say is the most important?

10. Would you like to know what our customers think our number-one, number-two, and number-three most important benefits are?

11. Would you like to know what our competitors think our most important benefits are?

The "Just Suppose" Question

This type of question is designed to reopen the customer's mind. The "just suppose" question will get your prospect to see beyond the immediate obstacle. The power of this type of question is in its ability to trigger the human imagination. This question gives your prospect or customer a fresh perspective. It broadens his or her mental vistas and horizons.

1. Just suppose I could get you one year of free maintenance—would that shift the balance in our favor?

2. I can't promise you this, but just suppose I could get you an extended warranty free of charge—would you be willing and able to buy this week?

3. Use your imagination, okay? Will you pretend that we can develop a chemical coating that will do everything you want it to do? What would you be willing to pay, per gallon, for such a coating?

4. Imagine that we can do all your corporate tax work, and prepare the 1040s for your senior executives, for the price you are now paying for just the annual audit. Are you interested in hearing more?

5. Just suppose I were able to have this hard-to-get model shipped in by air freight, for delivery next Tuesday—would you place your order today?

6. I've never heard of anything like that! But, just suppose we can custom-make it for you. Would you be willing to spend another $4,000 to get exactly what you want?

7. That's a very unusual color and interior combination you are asking for in that car. I don't know if I can find one like that or not, but suppose I can—do I have a promise from you that we'll get your business?

The Narrow-Down Question

Customers are often confused by the many choices that they need to make before they can actually decide on purchasing the right products for their needs. The narrow-down question helps simplify the decision-making process. Overwhelmed customers put off making decisions. They procrastinate. Use these questions to avoid this procrastination. When prospects have fewer choices, within reason, they can make decisions more rapidly and with less anxiety. Narrow-down questions limit confusion and keep your customers in a mental comfort zone.

1. If I had a magic wand and I could magically give you the home of your choice, which one would it be?

2. Is it a toss-up, or do you favor one of these? Which one?

3. Why don't we eliminate half of these right now, okay? Which half should we eliminate?

4. You've taken a lot of vacations in the past, haven't you? Of all those vacations, which ones were the most enjoyable and memorable? Should we concentrate on a vacation with those characteristics and benefits this year?

5. Most people are most interested in our _____ model. Is that model of interest to you?

6. You could spend $1,000 worth of your valuable time looking at all the options and all the choices. To save you time and money, what should we concentrate on?

7. Do you like to simplify your buying decisions? [Yes] Great! Can I show you how to simplify this purchase?

8.   Should we focus our presentation on just a few of the major benefits of our service or should we give a less-detailed but comprehensive view of everything we do? If you want us to concentrate on just a few major benefits, which ones should they be?

The Opinion Question

People's opinions are their world. Always respect the opinions and beliefs of your customers. By asking questions, you will learn what troublesome areas to avoid, and you will also learn all of your customers' hot buttons!

1. In your opinion, does this suggestion make sense for your company? Why or why not?

2. In your opinion, is quality or price more important in making a purchase decision like this?

3. Is your mind completely made up? Can you tell me how you arrived at your views?

4. What, in your honest opinion, is the greatest strength of our product? What, in your honest opinion, is the greatest weakness of our product?

5. What do you think your boss is interested in?

6. In your opinion, which company is number one in this field? Why?

7. Is today's cost-to-buy most important to you . . . or is cost-in-use?

8. In your opinion, what is the best way to sell a product like this?

9. In your opinion, is there any way we can get a larger percentage of your company's business? How?

10. Whose viewpoint do you think is more important in making this purchase decision—that of engineering or that of accounting?

11. In your view, is there any way we can get your legal department to approve this contract in less than two weeks? How?

12. Do you think everyone on the purchasing committee is being truthful with us?

13. Is there anything that scares you about making this decision? What?

14. Do you think we should concentrate on analyzing the past to avoid making mistakes again and again ... or should we look to the future to figure out how we can take advantage of new opportunities?

The Optimistic Question

The purpose of this question is to predict customers' positive responses. Use the power of the self-fulfilling prophesy. We tend to get what we think we will get. Optimistic questions will usually get optimistic answers.

1. You will be pleased to know that we have dropped the discount to 7 percent. Isn't that exciting?

2. I am positive that you won't mind a bit spending a few minutes with me to discuss this new financing plan, would you?

3. I am sure that you wouldn't have any objection to my making a copy of this specification sheet, would you ... if you knew it would help me serve you better?

4. Would you be pleased to learn we have lowered our interest rate?

5. Would it impress your boss to find out that you have bargained us down to the lowest price we have ever sold this for?

6. Would your family be happy to learn we are throwing in a free visit to Colombia with this trip to Panama?

7. I think you will be happy to learn that I can take you out to lunch at the restaurant of your choice, correct? Where shall we go to talk about this deal?

8. What would be the best outcome you could imagine from our meeting?

9. I have found you the home of your dreams. Are you ready to see it?

10. Wouldn't you like to take a trip you will remember for the rest of your life?

11. What would be the ideal length of our meeting? Are you pleased to know I will stay that long and not a minute longer?

12. What would it take to really amaze you in this field? Well, get ready. Our new product is all that and more. Would you like to see it?

The Pessimistic Question

By predicting a negative outcome, you may be able to get a positive response from your customers. You don't have to solve all problems by yourself. Many of your customers are eager to help you, so give them a chance. Pessimistic questions let your customers know the challenges you face. These questions are honest. They also create urgency and communicate your desire to get the business done soon! Don't be surprised if your customers shows you ways of speeding up the process of getting their business!

1. You are not interested in our once-a-year clearance prices, are you?

2. You aren't interested in using psychological testing to find more loyal salespeople, are you?

3. You wouldn't be interested in a bond paying 10 percent that is totally free of state and federal taxes, would you?

4. I don't suppose there would be any way we could squeeze a few extra dollars from the budget to get you the very best there is, or is there?

5. You don't have a guess about the budget for this, do you?

6. There is no way we can get you to reconsider, or is there?

7. You dislike foreign companies so much that I'll probably never be able to get any of your business, no matter how much money I could save you, correct?

8. Your factory has never been the first to add a new automation feature, and they are not going to break tradition now, are they?

9. You told me you only wanted a two-bedroom house and you won't consider a three-bedroom one now, or will you?

10. Your boss has never let you approve a purchase this large, and it is doubtful he will now, correct?

11. I'll probably never be able to compete against your friendship with that other salesman, no matter how much extra service I offer, right?

12. You just can't afford this quality level, can you?

The Polite Question

In an age when rudeness is the order of the day, this type of question will open doors for you wherever you go. People will like and respect you for your politeness. It is always safer to err on the side of being too polite rather than not being polite enough. These questions will also serve you well and bring you many benefits in your personal life!

1. You have been such a nice person to deal with. How was your company lucky enough to hire you?

2. I am sorry to ask you about this again, but could you tell me which features and benefits are most important to you?

3. May I put in a word to your boss on what an excellent job you have done researching these products?

4. I know you have to explain this to your boss. May I make your job a little easier by explaining it to him?

5. I know you have to justify this investment to your supervisor. Can I take that burden off your back and do it for you?

6. I know your job is very complex and that you have many things to think about. Instead of worrying about how you can sell your boss on this idea, why not let me do the hard work on it?

7. We originally scheduled this meeting to last one hour. Is that amount of time still available?

8. Did I tell you that you are one of the friendliest executive assistants I've met?

9. Pardon me, but would it be proper for me to ask which other companies we are competing with?

10. Would you be so kind as to tell me when you might be running out of supplies? Thank you, and if you don't mind my asking: When might you buy from us again?

The "Prime-the-Pump" Question

Even your most talkative customers occasionally run out of things to say. This type of question helps to avoid uncomfortable silent periods and can also be used to toss the conversational ball back to the customer if you run out of things to say or get tired of talking. These questions are an excellent way to ensure that the river of conversation does not run dry.

1. *Pretend I don't know anything about this, okay?* Give me as much detail as possible, will you?

2. That's fascinating. Would you mind telling me more?

3. Why did you lose some interest? What can I do to raise your level of interest?

4. What caused your level of increase to increase? How can I increase it even more?

5. Is that your opinion or someone else's? Whose?

6. What would he or she say about it?

7. What did you think of it before? What do you think of it today?

8. What is behind that statement?

9. Do you feel strongly about that? Why?

10. Is your mind made up? In what direction? Why?

11. Is there anything more you'd like me to know about your needs? Your views and opinions? Your likes and dislikes? What?

12.

I get the feeling I've talked too much, and I haven't let you talk enough. Is that true? Would you fill me in on what you have been thinking about?

13.

A mark of a good sales call is when the customer talks more than the sales representative. Did you know that? Will you enable me to make this a good sales call by having you talk more about how you feel about our products? Thank you!

The Pro-and-Con Question

These questions ask your prospect to look at both sides of the coin and to evaluate your idea objectively. Pro-and-con questions help you get an accurate picture of what your customer likes and dislikes about your product or service. These questions are one of the most accurate means of "temperature taking."

1. If you could get more of anything we offer, what would that be? Why? If you could get less of anything we offer, what would that be? Why?

2. *Please share with me your immediate emotional reactions.* What do you love and what do you hate? Why?

3. *Are the reasons for making this decision stronger than the reasons for not making it?* Can you tell me what both of those reasons are?

4. What is the number-one thing you like about our product? Why? What is the number-one thing you dislike about our product? Why?

5. It sounds like one part of you wants to do this and one part doesn't. Can you tell me about those parts of you and how they feel?

6. Let's be brutally honest. What stops you from buying now? Okay. What most interests you in buying?

7. *If you had to bet money on it,* would you say there are more votes for or against buying this machine? Why?

8. Can we make a trade? I'll buy you lunch if you tell me everything you like and everything you dislike about our product. Okay?

9. *In what ways are we stronger than the competition?* In what ways are we weaker?

10. Let's list all the positives and all the negatives of our product, okay? Now, what would it take to get you *to forget all the negatives*?

11. If you were me, what positive benefits of our products would you stress? What negatives would you point out? How would you deal with those?

The Rephrasing Question

The rephrasing question (sometimes called the paraphrasing question) is a must in every sales call. This questioning technique lets your customer know you are listening. It helps guarantee that you and your customer are on exactly the same wavelength. You can rephrase or repeat back either facts the customer has shared or his or her feelings and emotions.

1. You are confused? About what?

2. Does that mean this is a committee decision? Who is on the committee? What are their phone numbers?

3. This sounds very important! Can we cover it in a little more detail?

4. Are you saying you haven't really made your mind up yet? What would it take to help you make a decision?

CHAPTER 10

5. Are you saying you are frustrated? About what?

6. Are you saying you are really excited about this benefit? Great!

7. You have gotten the okay from the boss to go ahead? When?

8. Let's make sure we are talking the same language. When you say you want it "now," do you mean today or would next Monday be okay?

9. If I heard you correctly, you want your people trained in groups of 15 to 20 at one time, correct?

10. Are you saying you think it will be approved? When?

11. Are you saying this is urgent?

12. Let's make sure we are on the same wavelength: By credit, do you mean a line of credit or a lump sum payment?

13. I want to make sure I've got this exactly correct. Is that what you just said?

14. I didn't get all that down. Can you go over the specifications one more time? Thank you.

The Rhetorical Question

These questions help build a climate of agreement with your customer. They encourage the customer to continue to express his or her thoughts, ideas, and feelings, and keep the flow of conversation going. You can use them when you don't know what else to say. Rhetorical questions don't always have to be answered. Sometimes just a nod or a smile is all that is needed. These questions are friendly and build good feelings.

1. Isn't that the truth?

2. It sounds like we are in agreement, doesn't it?

3. What do you think?

4. That's a good question, isn't it?

5. Incredible, don't you think?

6. Who could argue with that?

7. May I have your opinion?

8. Aren't you glad you made the time to see this demonstration?

9. What about that?

10. Isn't this baby beautiful?

11. Don't you agree?

12. May I have your view?

13. What more could anyone ask for?

14. We're in the middle of the demonstration now, aren't we?

15. Can't you just see this working in your office?

16. You said you'd love this car, didn't you?

17. Everyone should have this service, right?

The Thought-Provoking Question

This type of question will direct your customer's thoughts toward the benefits of your product or service. Thought-provoking questions are also useful for opening up your customer's thinking or exploring new avenues and possibilities.

1. Can we throw some ideas around?

2. Can we brainstorm on this? Good!

3. Let your imagination go wild. What would a perfect product in our field be able to do? May I show you how our product nearly approaches perfection today?

4. Have you thought about how many hours of labor and how much overhead will be reduced once you automate with our computers? The savings could be gigantic! What do you think?

5. May I propose an idea that might startle you?

6. Are you willing to look at some radically new ways of solving your problems?

7. I've got a wild idea! Would you like to hear it?

8. What would you have to hear to get really excited about our product?

9. If you were head of our finance department, how would you finance this purchase?

10. If you worked in our engineering department, how would you improve our machine?

11. How much do you lose every time you lose an employee? Let's think about that and all the costs involved in getting a new person. Shouldn't you seriously look at purchasing some extra fringe benefits for your employees to keep them loyal and happy?

© Hisham Bharoocha

About the Author

A dual citizen of both Austria and the United States, Gerhard Gschwandtner is the founder and publisher of *Selling Power*, the leading magazine for sales professionals worldwide, with a circulation of 165,000 subscribers in 67 countries.

He began his career in his native Austria in the sales training and marketing departments of a large construction equipment company. In 1972, he moved to the United States to become the company's North American Sales Training Director, later moving into the position of Marketing Manager.

In 1977, he became an independent sales training consultant, and in 1979 he created an audiovisual sales training course called "The Languages of Selling." Marketed to sales manager at Fortune 500 companies, the course taught nonverbal communication in sales together with professional selling skills.

In 1981, Gerhard launched *Personal Selling Power*, a tabloid-format newsletter directed to sales managers. Over the years the tabloid grew in subscriptions, size, and frequency. The name changed to *Selling Power*, and in magazine format it became the leader in the professional sales field. Every year *Selling Power* publishes the "Selling Power 500," a listing of the 500 largest sales forces in America. The company publishes books, sales training posters, and audio and video products for the professional sales market.

Gerhard has become America's leading expert on selling and sales management. He conducts webinars for such companies as SAP, and *Selling Power* has recently launched a new conference division that sponsors and conducts by-invitation-only leadership conferences directed toward companies with high sales volume and large sales forces.

For more information on *Selling Power* and its products and services, please visit www.sellingpower.com.

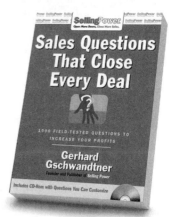

for any Sales Career

201 Super Sales Tips

The Pocket Sales Mentor

**The Pocket Guide to
Selling Greatness**

**The Ultimate Sales Training
Workshop**

**Secrets of Superstar
Sales Pros**

**The Art of Nonverbal
Selling**

Subscribe to *Selling Power* today and close more sales tomorrow!

GET 10 ISSUES – INCLUDING THE SALES MANAGER'S SOURCE BOOK.

In every issue of *Selling Power* magazine you'll find:

■ **A Sales Manager's Training Guide** with a one-hour sales training workshop complete with exercises and step-by-step instructions. Get a new guide in every issue! Created by proven industry experts who get $10,000 or more for a keynote speech or a training session.

■ **Best-practices reports** that show you how to win in today's tough market. Valuable tips and techniques for opening more doors and closing more sales.

■ **How-to stories** that help you speed up your sales cycle with innovative technology solutions, so you'll stay on the leading edge and avoid the "bleeding edge."

■ **Tested motivation ideas** so you and your team can remain focused, stay enthusiastic and prevail in the face of adversity.

Plus, you can sign up for five online SellingPower.com newsletters absolutely FREE.